The Family Business

A must-read for people deciding whether to step into the Father's business with their full lives, time, passions, and finances.

LAWRENCE TONG, international director, Operation Mobilisation

An enjoyable and discussable read; this book can help make Kingdom business *the* business of your home, group, church—and life.

EMILY SARMIENTO, president and CEO, Tearfund USA

This easy-to-read and engaging book acts as a great reminder of the invitation from Jesus to His followers to engage in the work of His father in every context we find ourselves in!

REVEREND NODDY SHARMA, head of church, schools and youth engagement, World Vision Australia

The Family Business invites readers into important questions and leads us to think about our lives—and our potential— with very readable and relatable insight.

REV. DR. PATRICK ODEN, director of academic integration and affiliate professor of theology, Fuller Theological Seminary

Get ready to be drawn in. This is a beautiful masterpiece you won't want to miss.

SHERRY SURRATT, geographical vice president of North America, OneHope

Mark Twain once said, "The two most important days in your life are the day you are born and the day you find out why." A quick and inspiring read, *The Family Business* by Geoff Peters is the kind of resource that can help you find your *why*. I wish I had this book when my career and family were just starting.

> **BARRY LANDIS**, chairman and cofounder, Ribbow Media Group, and executive director, The Briner Institute

Using a well-told, engaging story, Geoff paints a great picture of God's intent for humanity—to join Him in His Kingdom work on earth.

> **ANDREW SCOTT**, president and CEO, Operation Mobilization USA, and author of *Scatter: Go Therefore and Take Your Job with You*

The Family Business is a tale of spiritual legacy, personal volition, and future vision—timely for any believer who takes seriously the empowerment and equipping of the emerging generations.

> **REVEREND LISA PAK**, global strategy director, Finishing the Task

Geoff Peters gives us a parable that helps us recognize how powerful and personal the reality of our Kingdom mission is.

> **REV. DR. GLENN PACKIAM**, associate senior pastor, New Life Church, and author of *Blessed Broken Given*

Geoff Peters's parable of a family business is an apt metaphor. May we children of the good, good Father find ourselves in who He says we are and in the good works He prepared in advance for us to do.

TIM CROUCH, vice president for alliance missions, The Christian and Missionary Alliance

Geoff's story is a parable for our time, reminding us of the simplicity and power that come as we reflect on God's original design for His people.

JONATHAN THIESSEN, cofounder, Scatter Global

Geoff has written a modern-day parable that will make you sit down and rethink where you are as a person and where we are as a church toward God's family business.

EWOUT VAN OOSTEN, international director, TeenStreet

Geoff harnesses the power of fiction to help believers peel back the layers of their God-given purposes in this world.

LESA BROWN, founder and executive director, Awaken Creative Institute

We all know that we are called to be on mission with God, but most of the time we can't imagine what that looks like. If you need to be shown rather than told, then this story is for you!

JON HIRST, chief innovation officer at SIL and cofounder of Generous Mind

Parables are thought-provoking stories with intent, not just mindless entertainment. Sometimes they are life-changing. *The Family Business* is a well-written and engaging tale for a time such as this.

JAMES FERRIER, director of international operations, Community Bible Study

The Family Business offers a thought-provoking challenge to examine our lives to ensure we are directing our own strengths, gifts, and talents to do exactly what God made us to do.

GREG BAIRD, executive director, Outside the Bowl

THE FAMILY BUSINESS

A PARABLE
about Stepping
Into the Life You
Were Made For

GEOFF PETERS

Tyndale House Publishers
Carol Stream, Illinois

27   26   25   24   23   22   21
7   6   5   4   3   2   1

For Mason, Amanda, and baby—
Always do what He made you to do.
Love, Dad

CONTENTS

CHAPTER I

THE THREE OF US

JESSE LEANED ON THE CEDAR RAILING, gazing out over the rolling hills. Soft, glimmering rays of sunshine filtered through the early morning mist as a gray catbird swooped from the woodland beyond, its staccato whistles and squeaks forming a curious, melodious song. A smile formed on Jesse's face as he took in the wondrous beauty. He was so in the moment he hadn't noticed Holly was refilling his coffee cup.

"Glorious day, isn't it?" she asked softly.

"It is," Jesse agreed. "Is everything ready for the kids?"

"Yes." Holly nodded, her eyes brightening in excitement. "The beds are made and the bathrooms all have clean towels. I will be cooking today. Roast pork with applesauce for dinner! Is there anything else you'd like me to do?"

"Good . . . that's good," said Jesse. "I'll be in my office today, getting the paperwork ready. I've got to admit," he shared, "I'm a little nervous, Holly. I really want the kids to join me."

"I know that would make you very proud," Holly said, folding a blanket and draping it over the Adirondack chair. "But Jesse, you know that ultimately it's their choice. You've raised five kids who are as unique as can be, and they all love you dearly. They've always known in their hearts that this time would come, and a decision would be theirs to make. Who knows?" she suggested with a smile. "Your children may surprise you this weekend."

Jesse chuckled softly and walked back toward the house. "At my age, the excitement might just kill me." Stepping inside, he grabbed the handle of the door to steady himself as he looked back, adding, "Hey, Holly, if you made more coffee, I'm sure I'd enjoy another cup in a while."

Jesse walked toward his office, his posture strong and upright, not the least bit hunched with age. He entered his sun-filled study and took a deep breath. The scent of the floor-to-ceiling mahogany shelves and well-worn pages of his favorite books never ceased to please him.

Behind Jesse's commanding desk he stood for a moment, gazing at the room where he now spent so much of his time. He settled into his worn leather chair, the soft patina earned from years of faithful service. As he leaned back, he recalled the day he bought it. It was after his small hardware store in Ames had successfully turned a profit for one whole year. Jesse was young at the time, and the chair had been a big purchase for him. But in his mind, he figured he spent as much time sitting in his office with his ledger as he did stocking shelves and talking with customers, so he probably should have a proper chair to sit in while he did his bookkeeping.

In the beginning, Jesse created the hardware store so local farmers and families wouldn't have to make the trip from Ames to Des Moines when all they needed were a couple of bolts or blade-sharpening services. Jesse's farming family had raised him to work hard, and he didn't know any other way of life. He took that work ethic and poured it into Jesse's Hardware.

Over the decades, Jesse grew the small business into

a franchise that sprouted stores across the United States. He fondly touched the thick vellum map on his desk that marked all the locations of his stores. The edges of the map were slightly furled, and there were a few coffee stains in spots, but for the most part, the map was a clean representation of what Jesse had built. As he traced his fingers over each hardware store location, he thought about the owners who bought into the company, the employees who worked there, and the customers they served each day. Yes, each one of these stores and its people were a source of joy and pride for Jesse. His heart swelled as the names, faces, and stories of the Jesse's Hardware family rolled through his mind. Jesse was proud of what he had created, and he felt a deep love for everyone in the company.

Of course, he couldn't help but notice the empty spots on the map too. While his stores certainly spread across a great deal of land, there were gaps—in fact, more gaps than he had hoped to have at this stage. His fingertips wandered over the towns and cities that were not marked by a Jesse's Hardware hammer, and he couldn't help but feel sadness. These areas were holes in his master plan, and he needed help.

Jesse's vision for the future of his organization had

always been dependent on the participation of his children. His dream from the beginning, even before they were born, had been to involve his entire family in the business, full-time. Jesse was proud of each one of his children and could clearly see how their unique passions, skills, and personalities could be highly effective in his organization.

He also knew his vision would not be achieved at its current pace. Jesse needed to activate the next generation. The time had come for him to try to encourage his kids to join him.

It was Memorial Day weekend, and Jesse had invited all five of his children to come stay at the family estate for the three-day holiday. Jesse's housekeeper and faithful right hand, Holly, had been flitting around the house for weeks, making lists, shopping, baking cookies and muffins for the freezer, and doing everything she could to contain her building excitement.

"Time for a warm-up!" Holly sang out as she walked across Jesse's study with the coffee pot. "Would you like to go for a walk this morning? Beautiful day."

"Thank you, Holly, but I've got quite a bit to do here," said Jesse. "Maybe after lunch."

Holly refilled Jesse's coffee. "All right, but don't

forget to put your feet up if you're reading," she cautioned. "It helps the circulation in your legs."

As Holly returned to the kitchen with almost a skip in her step, Jesse chuckled, "Yes, yes, Miss H, I know."

Holly had been part of Jesse's family for about thirty years. In fact, she was in-residence, and had lived on the family estate for her entire adult working life. The love and admiration Jesse felt for Miss H—the name his children had coined for her when they were teenagers—ran deep. She was part of the fabric of his family.

As Jesse reclined in his chair, putting his feet up on the toadstool cushion under his desk, he recalled his first meeting with Holly at the Book Nook coffee shop back in 1990. Jesse had arrived in the late afternoon, and the coffee shop was nearly empty. The students from nearby Drake University were headed back to their dorms, backpacks in tow, and the professors were hours past their last cup of caffeine. As Jesse approached the front counter, he saw Holly sitting on the countertop reading a yellowed copy of *Paradise Lost* by John Milton. Jesse's sudden presence jolted her. She jumped down, offered an apology, and asked Jesse what she could get him. Jesse asked about Milton, and conversation followed as she poured his black coffee. "The story . . . it's everything!" gushed Holly. "There's good and evil, there's knowledge and power, there's rebellion and redemption. It's true to life." She continued, "Sure, it's hard to read, but it's so worth it."

Over the next hour, Jesse found out that Holly had been an English major at Drake. She knew she wanted to be a writer, but she also had to eat and make rent. So the job at the Book Nook was perfect. She could make enough to pay for a room near campus, and she had enough time to write. Plus, she had bottomless cups of free coffee and access to the bakery case.

When Jesse asked Holly what she liked to write, she blushed. "It's easy for me to wrap myself in other people's stories. I feel like that's my calling. It's not about me; it's about the beauty and pain that surrounds me . . . that surrounds us all."

As Jesse finished his coffee, he said to Holly, "My wife and I have five kids and could sure use some help around the house. We live just outside of Ames. I know you make good coffee, and I assume you know how to do laundry. If you're interested in housekeeping, we offer room and board, and I'll double what you make hourly here. I would just ask that you keep up your writing. You've got to pay attention to your gifts and use them. Too many people today lose sight of what they've got, or they get too busy to care. I don't want that to happen to you."

The very next week, Holly turned up at Jesse's family estate with two small suitcases and a leather satchel slung over her shoulder. She was twenty-three. Days became weeks, which became years. Time carried on, and Holly earned a beloved place within Jesse's family. She became fast friends with his wife, Emma, and doted on the kids like they were her own. When she wasn't cooking or cleaning or playing quick games of Uno with whoever was begging for attention, Holly could be found in a small study Jesse created for her up in the attic. It was a warm, cozy spot with a picture window overlooking the sweeping grounds of the family home and the wood-land forest beyond. Soft, moss-green carpet and walls painted in a buttery shade made the space a writing sanctuary, a soothing spot with just the right lighting for Holly to clear her mind and write.

Over the years, Holly was prolific at her writing desk. Each time she completed a manuscript, she tied it up carefully with a white grosgrain ribbon, making a neat bow on top. The shelves in Holly's attic were lined with these ornate paper stacks, representing a slow but steady manifestation of her life's work. Of course, she would tell you it was not her writing that was important; it was the stories themselves that carried importance.

As a natural observer—a witness—of humanity, Holly would tell you it was Jesse and Emma who were doing the vital stuff of life. She wouldn't even be there without them! In her mind, she was just the housekeeper who cared for the children and worked to keep the family safe. Writing was her way of keeping everything straight.

Over the years, as it goes with families, the kids moved out one by one, on a quest to start their own lives. It started with Evie, Jesse and Emma's oldest child. Evie was a classic firstborn, headstrong and smart. After graduating at the top of her high school class, she headed for Drake University, Holly's alma mater, the month before her eighteenth birthday. Her debate skills were finely tuned at that point (a fact Jesse and Emma could attest to), and she thought perhaps a law degree would be in her future.

The following year Dave left. With just his guitar case, a canvas backpack, and a plaid bucket hat, Dave was off, headed to the University of Michigan in pursuit of a future in psychology.

Next Zach became an Iowa State Cyclone. Jesse and Emma's funny middle child was content to stay close, not straying beyond the perceived safety and comfort of Ames and the family home.

Becca followed her big brother to Iowa State, claiming their School of Education was the strongest in the Midwest. Of course, everyone in the family knew she just wanted to be close to Zach.

And finally, Mo—the baby of the family who had been just four years old when Holly moved in—packed his percussion instruments, skateboard, and oversize rucksack into his Camry in late August 2004, headed for Colorado State University. Mo's little blue Toyota sped down the tree-lined driveway, and Jesse, Emma, and Holly stared at the dust cloud long after the car was gone.

With each child's departure, those left behind responded a little differently. Jesse took each of his children into his arms, embracing them in a way that both protected them and gave them the confidence to know they were being released into the world. Emma, on the other hand, helped them pack their bags, talking with them about their hopes and fears, reassuring them in moments of confusion, and hiding little gifts in their luggage to make sure they remembered just how loved they were. As for Holly, she stood at a distance, and through her tears and love and well wishes, sent a little bit of her heart with them for the journey.

The first few weeks after Mo left home, it was business as usual for Jesse. He was still serving as CEO of his company and had his sights set on ambitious growth. He had no plans to slow down. Emma continued with her charities and community outreach activities. She was the type of person who stowed bags in her car filled with cash and essentials for homeless people. Beyond handing out the bags, Emma would often buy people lunch so they could sit together, share a meal, and talk. Emma always made time for people—even when she didn't appear to have much time to give. She was a lover of everyone, and now, with the kids gone, she had more time than ever to reveal her true nature.

On the other hand, Holly wasn't feeling quite as confident with her new role. Over coffee one morning, Emma broached the tender subject. "Life isn't quite what it used to be, is it?" she asked with a wistful smile. "But Holly, my dear, this is a great gift. We've got to use the time we have, not focus on the past. The open road is ahead!" Emma's attempt to cheer her along wasn't lost on Holly. She was grateful for Emma's loving spirit and encouragement.

The following weeks and months brought a new rhythm to the estate. Emma and Holly lived and worked more fluidly than ever before. When Holly was dusting the bookshelves in Jesse's office, Emma would jingle a bell playfully in the doorway, beckoning Holly to stop and sit with her for tea and cookies. And when Emma was packing canned goods for the local food pantry, Holly would turn on ABBA so she could tap and twirl with jars of sliced peaches in her hands.

The two women grew closer as time went on. Within months of Mo's departure, the energy and passion that once had been focused on the children was now directed outwardly, further than before. The women both glowed, each in her own way, as they collectively embraced this new chapter in their lives. Despite his relentless schedule running the business, even Jesse noticed the change in the household. "Whatever you two are cooking up all day long," Jesse would say, "keep doing it. Our home is alive!"

Emma's passion to love and serve others was not just swelling, it was spilling out over the edges of her life. She brought Holly along to help her love and care for the elderly, the sick, and the poor. When Emma spoke to someone who was hurting, the connection was palpable. People felt loved and understood by Emma. And they felt at peace with Holly. Together, the two were a dynamic force for good in the community.

Their relationship grew sweeter over time too. A few times a week, Emma would leave handwritten notes under Holly's door, proclaiming, "Today is a writing day! Do what you were made to do!" So when Holly heard the rustle of paper sliding under her door as the sun peeked through the edges of her window shade, a smile would spread across her face.

The years went by, and while the big, bustling family gathered for all the major holidays, birthday celebrations, and college graduations dotted throughout the calendar, the days in between were fairly quiet for the trio—quiet yet purposeful.

In early January 2018, Emma and Holly sat down to plan a party. Jesse would be turning seventy in March, and they wanted to throw a huge celebration, inviting the whole family and all of their friends. Over the cold, dark weeks that followed, the spirits of the women were buoyed by the party. There were invitations and menus to plan, decorations to design, and waitstaff to organize. It would be a huge gala for Jesse.

As February neared, Holly couldn't help but notice Emma was tired. Initially she chalked it up to Emma's faithful community work combined with preparations for Jesse's birthday party, but her exhaustion seemed to be progressing quite rapidly. Her rosy glow was fading, and as the three sat around the table for dinner, Emma appeared to be eating less and less. Holly saw her once energetic friend frequently drawn to her easy chair, gazing out the window with a painfully furrowed brow, a mohair blanket pulled up to her chin.

Holly tried to encourage Emma to visit a doctor. "Something's not right," Holly urged. "Please call and make an appointment?"

After weeks of prompts and nudges, Emma finally made an appointment. "I'll go with you," Holly said, touching her arm. Emma smiled appreciatively at her friend.

As they walked to the front door of the clinic, Holly reached for Emma's hand. "I'm here," she said. "I'm always here for you. You know that, don't you?"

Emma nodded.

Once inside, the nurse called Emma's name. The

two women walked together, hand in hand, toward the examination room. After a brief conversation with the doctor, a blood test, and an endoscopic ultrasound, the doctor told Emma she could go home. "We will call you when we have your results," he assured her.

The drive home was quiet. As Holly gripped the wheel, Emma looked out the window at the passing cornfields, scattered with old stalks and mounds of melting snow. She knew in her heart this would be her last winter. She also knew she was at peace with it. She had lived a good life and tried to love everyone she could. This life was finite, and her time had come. Hopefully the seeds she had planted in those she loved would grow and flourish.

Days later, Emma received a call. The doctor said he was sad to report it was stage 4 pancreatic cancer. Emma hung up the phone and shared the news with Jesse and Holly. Jesse pulled Emma close, his rough weathered hands gently reassuring her without the need for words. Holly placed her hands on Emma's small shoulders and rested her head on Emma's back as they all wept. After a few moments, Emma gathered herself, brushed her hands down the front of her skirt, and wiped the tears from her face. "This is what's meant to be," she said. "I know that. And before I die, I still have things to do."

Emma didn't stop her community outreach activities in the coming weeks, and she proudly stood beside Jesse on the night of his seventieth birthday party. The whole family was there, along with many of their lifelong friends and some of Jesse's dearest employees. Emma beamed with pride as she looked out at everyone who had gathered there that evening. This collective group was so unique, so diverse, and yet in spite of their differences, they were united by a single thread that Jesse had started long, long ago. It was a thread of many strands that connected Emma and Holly, the children, and all of their friends and associates. Yes, they had all been carefully, artfully, lovingly woven together into this single grand tapestry.

That night, Emma could have gone on forever. She tried to cajole her friends and family to stay and have one more glass of champagne, dance to one more song, or eat one last shrimp toast, but by midnight the last coats had been taken from the closet, and the final car pulled away.

In mid-April, before the snowdrops poked their white heads through spring's final patches of snow,

Emma slipped away. Her final days had been filled with anguish as blood from her pancreas stained the corners of her mouth and marked her crisp, white sheets. The children took turns weeping mournfully as they sat with their mother for what would surely be the last time. Between visits, Holly read to Emma, whispering prayers of strength into her ear. Jesse stood in the doorway, his face wracked with pain.

After Emma took her last breath, Holly and Jesse looked at one another, flooded with a mix of grief and relief. Emma would no longer have to suffer. It was finished.

CHAPTER 2

AN OPEN INVITATION

"HOW ABOUT THAT WALK?" Holly asked gently as Jesse finished his sandwich. "We have time before the kids arrive."

"Okay, okay, let's walk," Jesse replied.

The two headed down the driveway, strolling under the canopy of silver maples flanking the pavement. The spring sun was strong, flickering through the leaves and making their cheeks flush pink with warmth.

"It's good the kids are coming," Jesse said, his voice laden with hope. "It will give me the chance to tell them what I see in each of them . . . to let them know I really need them in the business."

"Why, you and I both tell them all the time what they have to offer the world, Jesse! They know you love them dearly," assured Holly. "But you're right, this is another good opportunity to remind them."

"I really need them with me, Holly. Our leadership team needs them. Heck, the whole company needs them if we're going to move ahead with our expansion plans," Jesse insisted.

As they reached the end of the property's fence line, Holly saw a gray catbird sitting on one of the posts. It stared at them with utter disinterest. "What do you say we get back to the house?" Holly suggested. They turned around, Holly looping her arm through Jesse's as she looked over her shoulder to see the bird still staring blankly at them.

Back at the house, while Holly finished arranging flowers on the table, Jesse walked up the long staircase to his bedroom. He put on his best sports coat, changed his shoes, gargled, and put a splash of aftershave on his face. As he was walking back down the stairs, he heard a car door slam and the front door open.

Jesse made it to the foyer in time to see his son, Dave, hang up his coat. Jesse immediately stretched out his arms, beckoning Dave for a hug. "Come here, my boy!" exclaimed Jesse. "It's good to see you. How was the drive?"

"It was smooth, Dad! I hope you don't mind I brought my guitar since we're staying until Monday," he said, motioning toward the guitar case on the floor.

"Not at all, not at all. You'll have to play something for us," Jesse said with a smile.

Just then the door opened again. "Dad! Your favorite son is here!" shouted Zach with a quick wink as he eyed his brother Dave.

"Aha! Zach!" Jesse grabbed him by the shoulders and gave him a hearty embrace. "Welcome, welcome. I know Holly can't wait to see you boys," said Jesse. "Holly, Dave and Zach are here!"

"And Eeeevieeee!" bellowed Evie dramatically as she opened the door and dropped her blue leather bags at her feet. "Daddy!" she squealed, taking short, quick steps in her high heels as she gave Jesse a kiss on the cheek. "How are you? Are you ready for a big party weekend? Can you keep up with us?" Evie teased, as she elbowed Zach in the ribs.

"I'll do my best, Evie!" Jesse answered with a smile. "I'm so glad you're here, sweetie. Boys, help Evie with her bags."

Zach rolled his eyes at Evie as he and Dave dutifully picked up her bags, carrying them toward the staircase.

"Thank you kindly, boyzzzz," Evie murmured, sarcasm dripping from her voice.

"Hey, Miss H!" shouted Zach and Dave as they met Holly in the hallway.

"Oh, my boys!" cooed Holly, taking one in each arm for a three-person embrace. As if on cue, the boys lifted Holly off the floor and gently put her back down. "You two!" Holly beamed. "Oh, I think I hear Evie," she added. "Shoot! I forgot to pull her favorite cheese out of the fridge so it would be room temp!"

"Oh no!" Zach mouthed to Dave, a feigned look of concern on his face.

The boys and Evie joined Jesse in the living room. Holly walked in with dishes of nuts and olives, placing them on the coffee table. "So, Dave," Jesse asked, settling into his wingback chair, "what's happening at work?"

Dave leaned back, resting his elbow on the arm of the sofa. "Nothing new, Dad. The practice is doing well. I have a full slate of clients. Everyone has things they need to talk about and process . . . that's never going to change. I guess that means job security for me."

"Any real crazies that you have to deal with?" inquired Evie, leaning in. "Any women who admit they are slowly poisoning their husbands?"

"No, nothing exciting like that," Dave said with a smile. "Just a lot of people who are sad. Some who don't feel there's a reason they exist. Others who are in conflict and need help navigating relationships."

"Ugh. Boring," Evie huffed.

"Dave, I have no doubt you are an excellent therapist," Jesse affirmed. "You're an attentive listener and have the unique ability to understand people's pain."

As Holly made last-minute preparations in the kitchen, voices came from the foyer. "And then I had to crush the corn puff in his nose so he could sneeze it out and breathe again!"

"Fam-i-lyyyy!" Becca shouted from the doorway. "We're here!" Becca and Mo walked into the living room, Becca throwing her coat over the chair and heading straight for Holly. "Hi, Miss H!" she gushed, giving Holly a big hug.

"Hey, everyone," Mo said, ambling over to the sofa. "What's happening?"

"It sounded like Becca was regaling you with another one of her fascinating tales from the kindergarten chronicles, Mo," Zach smirked. "Becca, how many boogers did you watch five-year-olds eat this week?"

"Listen, I might be raising up a future CEO or world leader, Zach. Not everyone can be a cool marketing director like you," Becca shot back with a smile.

Zach grabbed his chest as if he had been punched.

"Mo," Jesse said, "What's the latest at Squash?"

"We have a lot of exciting things happening, Dad," Mo said earnestly. "Our food mobile tests in Keokuk and Burlington were a big success, and we've received a grant to launch them throughout some of the lowest income cities in the Midwest. We're starting in Missouri and Nebraska for phase one and will be rolling out to Illinois, Indiana, and Ohio in phase two."

"Mo! I'm so proud of you!" Jesse beamed. "Feeding the poor is a noble enterprise, Son."

Jesse sat back, casting his eyes toward the ceiling, deep in thought. "You've turned out to be quite the leader," he reflected.

Mo shifted in his seat uncomfortably, getting up to join Holly. "Hi, Miss H," Mo said softly. "I haven't given you a hug yet."

"Mo, it's so good to see you," Holly said as she embraced Mo. "What can I get you, hon?"

As the family chatted, Holly refilled glasses and replenished snacks as she quietly relished all the energy in the room. Her heart was full.

At seven o'clock, Holly rang the dinner bell—the one she had used regularly when the kids were still living at home, but which was now used only for occasions such as this.

When everyone was seated in the dining room, Jesse stood at the head of the table and tapped his glass with his knife. "Kids! Kids! I'd like to propose a toast," he declared, clearing his throat. "To family. Each one of you is loved more than you'll ever know by me and Holly, and of course, your mother," he closed his eyes for a moment and bowed his head. "May each of you use your unique gifts and talents to bless the world."

"Cheers!" the kids all said, raising their glasses in unison.

"What's for dinner, Miss H?" asked Mo.

"I smell pork!" Zack snorted, making oinking sounds.

Holly laughed as she carved the roast. "Oh, Zach," she sighed. "What would we do without you?"

"Our family's cumulative IQ would go way up, that's for sure!" teased Becca. "Hey, Holly, how long did you roast the pork? I'm having a dinner party in a few weeks, and this would be perfect."

"Well, my agency is hosting a launch party for Burberry's winter handbag collection, and I want to serve this wine!" Evie added. "Holly, where is this Pinot Noir from?"

As everyone filled their plates and the dinner conversation ensued, Holly kept a close eye on the food and her family. She knew each child's strengths, weaknesses, and ongoing battles. She knew what brought them joy and pain. She couldn't help but wonder how they would react to Jesse's impending invitation.

When the last of the silverware was laid to rest on its plate, Jesse took a deep breath and placed his elbows on the table, leaning in toward the kids. "Did everyone get enough to eat?" Jesse asked earnestly.

As the kids all responded in the affirmative with nods and sighs, Jesse said, "Good, good. Well, as you may have guessed, I brought you here for more than just a family weekend. I want to talk with you about your lives and your futures."

"Dom, dom, dom!" Zach bellowed in a foreboding tone.

Jesse smiled at Zach. "No, no, this is not a dark

discussion, Zach. On the contrary, I want to talk business with you."

Jesse leaned back in his chair and started to smile. "The company is doing really well. We have experienced some flatlines and even a few downturns, but if you look at the full lifetime of the company, our trajectory remains positive. Of course, as you kids know, I have a pretty big vision. Some analysts outside of the company tell me there's no way I can achieve the growth I'm aiming for. Others tell me I shouldn't even try, and that I'm nothing. Throughout my life, there have also been those who have tried to thwart me by putting roadblocks in the company's way. But despite our setbacks and challenges, I can see it, kids. We can do this," Jesse rallied, standing up from the table. "We can make Jesse's Hardware a household name. A place folks can turn to when they need help with the basics of living. A brand people can trust for good tools and trusted advice. In fact, I envision a day when Jesse's Hardware is on the tip of the tongue of everyone, everywhere!"

Jesse paused, a look of deep satisfaction on his face.

"And that is one of the reasons I've invited you here this weekend. You see, I want you to join the family business. I want you to take the skills and talents you possess—the things that make you, you—and I want you to invest those things in the company.

"I know, I know. I can just hear you now. 'But Dad, why do I have to give up my life for you?' Let me assure you, I don't want you to give up your life for the company. Not at all. I want you to *bring* your life to the company. All of it. Every single aspect of your life.

"You see, this company is not just any old entity. You were born into this family, and that means the company is in your DNA. As much as you might like to compartmentalize it—enjoying it and the benefits of it when you like and putting it back in a box on the shelf when you don't—at some point you are going to have to face the reality that the company is part of you.

"It has always been my dream that you kids would be a part of what I've created. You are all gifted in your own ways, and each of you has something to offer . . . something the company needs."

Holly gently eased the ensuing silence by walking around the table, refilling water glasses.

"I'm not asking for a response tonight, or even this weekend," Jesse assured the kids. "I know this is a lot to chew on. And I know it's going to require some processing. I just ask that you be open-minded and that you talk to me about any concerns you have. I am here for you."

Jessed exhaled triumphantly, "Okay, I've planted the seed, Holly! Now let's have some of that strawberry shortcake I saw in the fridge!"

The atmosphere in the room was more subdued as Holly spooned the dessert into dishes. Mo looked pensive as he tapped his dessert spoon on the tablecloth. Becca chatted with Evie, inquiring playfully how she could get her hands on one of those limited-edition Burberry handbags. As Evie responded she twirled her hair on her index finger, her thoughts clearly on something other than leather accessories. Zach's knee bounced under the table as he tried to come up with a joke to break the tension. And Dave just took it all in, absorbing the energy from his siblings and father.

⚒

Saturday morning, Holly put platters of muffins, bagels, and toast on the table, along with plates of fresh fruit and a tray of bacon. "Who wants an omelet or scrambled eggs?" she asked brightly as everyone sat down.

"Just coffee for me, Holly," said Evie sleepily. "It's too early to eat."

"Evie, it's 10 a.m.!" exclaimed Becca. "By now I'd have already been at school for three hours!"

Evie clapped silently for Becca, a wry smile on her face.

"I'd love some eggs, Miss H!" said Zach.

"I would, too, please," Dave chimed in. "Whatever way you want to cook them, I'll eat them."

As Holly cooked eggs in the kitchen, she could hear Jesse say, "All right, kids. Last night I gave you a lot to think about. Today let's have some fun. What do you say we go out for a spin?"

"Yesssssss!" exclaimed Zach. "I thought you'd never ask." He and Dave executed a mock high-five from opposite sides of the table.

After breakfast, the family put on their jackets and boots and gathered outside the barn. "Okay, figure out who wants an ATV and who wants a Gator, and let's ride!" Jesse exclaimed.

Evie and Zach each made a beeline to an ATV. Dave sauntered over to a Gator and waved his arm, motioning for Becca and Mo to join him. Jesse stood back, observing his brood. He walked over to an ATV and strapped on his helmet. "Alright, kids. Show me what you've got!" Jesse shouted over the roar of the engines.

The four vehicles burst out from the barn doors, destined for the fields beyond. Holly stood on the back deck, leaning on the railing while she sipped her tea. She could hear squeals, hoots, and hollers as Jesse and the kids tore up the property, catching air over small hills and racing each other along the straightaways.

She smiled as she saw the Gator stop at the brush line. Mo was leaning out, touching something on the ground. No doubt he had seen a flower or mushroom he wanted to investigate. Holly could see Dave was driving the Gator—yes, Dave was probably the only one who would have stopped to satisfy Mo's curiosity. Well, maybe Becca would have. But only if she wasn't competing with the others. Becca never liked losing.

Evie and Zach were neck and neck, battling for first place in the stretch along the cornfields. Holly could barely watch. As the firstborn, Evie just couldn't accept second place. Ever. And Zach had been burdened from birth, it seemed, with a need to impress others. Holly wondered if it was simply middle child syndrome, or if it was something deeper.

Jesse's hearty laugh bellowed across the property as he sat on the top rung of the split-rail fence. He had parked his ATV and was in his element, enjoying his children and the bounty of his life's work. As Holly thought of Jesse's master plan, she wondered how he would bring it to fruition. She would surely do her part and try to encourage the children to participate in the business, but in the end, it was up to each of them. It was their decision.

Back at the house, Jesse and the kids all swarmed the kitchen. Holly had put out a basket of bread, platters of meats and cheeses, and almost anything a person could want on a sandwich.

"So, Becca, what's Marty going to say when you tell him you want to give up your cushy teaching job and start working for the family business?" teased Zach.

"I don't know, Zach," replied Becca. "What's Zoey going to say when you tell her you're going to get a big boy job, you know, like one where you actually have to use your brain?"

"Kids, that's enough," Jesse said gently but firmly.

"I know I gave you a lot to think about. I don't expect you to give me a decision this weekend. I want you to go home and think about it. Take the summer. Really think hard. Then let's all get back together here on Labor Day weekend, and you can tell me what you've decided."

Evie poured wine in a juice tumbler and said, "Well, I don't have to think long and hard about it. I'm in. 100 percent. In."

She saw Mo staring intently at her wine and said, "What? Just because we're Iowan doesn't mean I can't introduce a little European culture to this family. If we were having lunch in Paris, we'd be drinking wine."

Mo looked away, clearly uninterested in Evie's digression.

"How did you arrive at your decision, Evie?" asked Mo.

"Well, I'm smart . . . shut up, Zach," Evie interrupted herself, as Zach innocently threw his hands in the air. "I work hard, I've worked my whole life in public relations, and I know how to help companies develop strong, positive brands. I am confident I can take Jesse's Hardware to the next level."

"*You* can take Jesse's Hardware to the next level? So, it's not really about helping Dad, but more about pushing him aside so you can achieve your vision?" Becca inquired, tucking potato chips into her sandwich.

"No, not at all, but thanks for letting us know how you feel, Becca," Evie retorted, swirling the wine in her tumbler. "I'm just saying I know I have a lot to offer, and I'm willing to do it for Dad."

"I don't think Becca meant to be so harsh, did you, Becca?" asked Dave.

"Actually, . . ." Becca started.

"Well, as for me, I'm not sure," Dave said, speaking over Becca, more to prevent an argument than to steal the floor. "I feel like I'm making a difference where I am. I have a pretty solid therapy practice. I'm in a band and get to play my guitar almost every weekend . . ." Dave ran his fingers through his curly dark hair. "I'm just really content and not sure about this kind of change."

"Dave, be honest," Zach piped in. "You just aren't ready to give up the ladies yet, are you? We all know your weekend gigs are more about the mamas than the music. Amiright?"

Dave blushed. "Whatever, Zach. I'm just trying to say I don't know."

Jesse interjected, "Dave, Son, I understand this is a big ask. That's why I'm giving you the summer to think about it. Take the time. Do some soul-searching."

"Well, Dad, I'll have to think about it too," said Zach. "I'm not sure I can give up all the great bennies I have at the marketing firm. I mean, I get client lunches at all the best restaurants, a corporate gym, 401K matching, four weeks of paid vacation . . . it would just be a lot to give up. I mean, I know we haven't talked brass tacks with you and what the company can offer . . . I'm just thinking out loud."

"Oh, does that make your brain hurt?" snipped Becca. "You'd be lucky to work for Dad. The trouble for you is that you'd actually have to start working."

"Geez, Becca, did you have a cup of bitters for breakfast?" replied Zach, clearly hurt. "Evie, when Becca joins Dad's company, definitely don't put her on your PR team. She would suck at it."

Becca exhaled. "Sorry, Zach," she said, her tone softening. "I'm just a little stressed right now. I didn't mean to take it out on you. Forgive me?"

"Sure, Becca, sure," Zach said, his eyes still downcast.

"As for me," Becca said, smiling weakly, "I don't know. I live a pretty quiet life. Marty and Hannah are my focus. I have all major holidays and my summers off. If I joined the company, it would completely change my life. I'm good at picking out curtains, not helping run a massive enterprise."

She added, "Dad, your life is very public, and people can be so mean. We've all seen the way people attack your character. I'm not as strong as you are. I like living in anonymity."

Jesse listened thoughtfully, and with a slow, compassionate nod, he turned to Mo.

"M-hmm," Mo said, clearing his throat. "I just don't know that the company is my thing. I mean, I appreciate it, and I love you, Dad, but I'm not so sure that your business needs to be my business—or my life's work, for that matter. I say that with all due respect."

"Sure, Mo, I hear you, Son," said Jesse. "Well," he continued, slapping his thighs as he stood up, "I think this was good. You started to put your initial thoughts out there, and I appreciate that. I just want to urge you not to stay there. If you dig beneath the surface of your gut reactions, you'll find there's more to discover about yourself."

"Sure, Dad," the kids all chimed in as they stood up to clear their plates. From where she stood in the butler's pantry, Holly could feel something in the air. It wasn't necessarily dark, nor was it light. It was an unknown quantity.

The mood at dinner that night was decidedly brighter. Becca had made up with Zach by letting him win during their afternoon card game and then loudly proclaiming how brilliant he was to everyone in the room. It appeared Dave had all but forgotten about being outed by Zach. Then again, with Dave, you never truly knew what was going on inside his head. Evie grabbed the reins on the evening vibes by trying to teach everyone how to do the shuffle. As the kids danced, their laughter filled the kitchen. Holly poured all of her love into the family meal.

"Holly!" exclaimed Jesse. "The chicken smells absolutely out of this world."

"Thank you," Holly said as she placed it on the table. "You've all had this once before. But you liked it so much, I decided to make it again." Everyone started passing the dishes around the table, loading up their plates.

"No one can cook like Holly!" Zach cheered. "Even you, Martha Stewart," he said, pointing a finger at Becca.

"All right, let's keep the good times rolling," said Evie. "Let's play a game during dinner. How about 'Never Have I Ever.'"

"Wow, Evie, are we in middle school now?" chided Becca.

"Well, now that our resident pedagogue Becca has spoken up, I think we all can agree that we absolutely should stoop to our seventh-grade selves and play this game," Evie declared. "Miss H, do you have any of those oyster crackers you used to give us when we were sick?"

"Of course!" Holly said, "I always keep a spare bag in the pantry. You never know when someone may not feel well."

As Holly went to retrieve the crackers, Evie relayed the rules. "Everyone gets a pile of crackers. Whenever a statement is read out loud, if you have done it, put a cracker in front of you. If you haven't, sit still. When you have ten crackers in front of you, you're out. The last person to still be playing is the winner. Got it?"

As Holly distributed piles of crackers at each person's place, Evie continued, "Since we don't have an actual game, I'll ask the questions and we'll all answer. It's the honor system, people. No lying allowed. Okay?

"All right, question 1. Never have I ever snooped through someone's bedroom or bathroom without them knowing."

Evie looked around the room, watching her brothers and sister. Becca, Zach, and Dave all slid a cracker in front of them. Evie followed.

"Question 2. Never have I ever been physically hurt trying to impress someone."

Zach, Evie, and Becca moved a cracker.

"Question 3. Never have I ever tried to get out of a speeding ticket by flirting or crying."

Evie and Becca added a cracker. Zach started to push one forward and then stopped. "Well, to be accurate, I wasn't crying to get out of it. I was legitimately crying. I don't think that counts."

"Question 4. Never have I ever had a crush on a friend's parent."

Evie, Dave, Zach, and Becca added a cracker to the pile. "Oooh, who did you have a crush on, Dave? Was it Luke's mom? She was on fire!" said Zach. Dave pretended to zip his lips shut, not saying a word. "Aw, you're no fun," complained Zach.

"Okay, order in the court!" said Evie. "Here is question 5: Never have I ever shoplifted."

The siblings all looked at each other around the table. Slowly, Evie pushed a cracker forward. "What?" she asked in a cocky tone as Zach and Becca laughed. "It was a lip gloss in high school. I'm not proud of it."

"Evie, can we just enjoy our dinner without the games?" asked Mo.

"Well, Mo, I think you'd be enjoying yourself more

if you had even one cracker in your pile," Evie teased. "I guess now we all know who the prude is."

"Okay, Mo, we'll do one more," said Evie. "This one's for you. Question 6: Never have I ever had hate in my heart for a member of my family."

"Hate? That's a tough word, Evie," said Dave. As the siblings looked around the table, Mo's face began to turn red. He lifted up his fist and slammed it down on the pile of crackers, crushing them into tiny pieces.

Mo promptly stood up and excused himself from the table. "I'm sorry, Dad. Miss H, the dinner was beautiful. I'll see you all in the morning." And with that, Mo was gone.

"Whoa, Evie," Zach murmured.

"Well, if we're all going to work together in the company," said Evie, "I thought we should have everything on the table. I guess Mo isn't a fan of transparency."

Jesse, who had been quiet throughout dinner, spoke up. "Kids, I understand you wanting some fun and games, but I also want to remind you that as a family, we build each other up; we don't tear each other down. Evie, if you asked that question in innocence, then we'll leave it at that. But if your motives weren't as pure, I'd ask you to reflect on that."

Because Jesse rarely chided his adult children, his words were received solemnly.

"Yes, Dad," Evie murmured.

The next morning was Sunday, and Sunday on the estate meant two things: church and lunch out. The kids all got up for the 10:30 a.m. service at Grace Church in Ames. As they sat together, occupying the same pew they had as children growing up, they couldn't help but feel comfortable. The songs were the same, the offering basket hadn't changed, and by all appearances, the pastor hadn't changed his suit, either.

After church, Jesse took the whole family out for lunch at Hickory Park. When the food was served, Jesse asked, "Hey Mo, do you mind blessing our meal?"

"Sure, Dad," Mo said. "Happy to."

Bowing his head, Mo said, "Jesus, thank You for this day and for the opportunity to be in Your house to hear Your Word. Our family has been blessed beyond measure by You, and we just ask for Your guidance as we decide how to best live our lives in a way that honors You and contributes to Your work here on earth. In Your name we pray, amen."

As everyone dug into their burgers and fries, Holly said, "So, does anyone have any big plans this summer?"

"Marty, Hannah, and I are going on a road trip when school is out," said Becca. "We're planning to drive out West and maybe do some camping and hiking. Hannah is the perfect age for that kind of trip. It'll be something she'll remember forever."

"That's great, Becca," said Zach. "Zoey and I are planning to visit her parents out East. I'm not sure when we're going, but we'll try to take a few extra days to stay on the coast in Rhode Island if we can."

"Well, I don't have any plans other than hot yoga classes and maybe some online dating," said Evie.

"Are you in the market again?" asked Dave.

"Yep!" declared Evie. "I've been divorced for a year. I sat Shiva way longer than I needed to."

"Ha!" said Zach. "Like you didn't go on any dates last year? Really? You expect us to believe that?"

Evie shrugged.

"Any desserts today?" the waitress asked.

"Ooooh!" whispered Becca.

"Ma'am, we'll have hot fudge sundaes all around," said Jesse.

"Yessssss!" said Zach, leaning in to Becca.

When the last spoon rested in its sundae glass, the

family headed back to the family estate, where they played cards, read, and napped for the afternoon.

Dinner that night was the most peaceful of the weekend. The bickering and bitterness seemed to have melted away as everyone chatted around the table.

"Hey, Dave," Mo said. "We're having a benefit this July to raise money for our food mobiles. Any chance you and your band could play at it? It'll be in Des Moines. I can pay you, but probably not as much as you get for your regular gigs."

"Yeah, Mo, I'd love to help you," Dave replied. "I'll talk to the guys. I'm sure we can work something out."

As the kids talked, Jesse stared at his plate, twirling his linguini on his fork. How could he make sure the kids knew just how much he loved them? How could he convey how necessary they were to the family business? What would it take to break through?

As if she heard his inner thoughts, Holly spoke up, "Kids, I just want you to know how excited your dad was for this weekend. As his right-hand helper, so to speak, I can tell you with confidence that each of you is so important to him. And if I could be so bold," Holly said hesitantly, "I would tell you that while he desperately wants you to join him in the company, he also wants this decision to be your choice. He doesn't want you to be coerced or shamed into it. It's important that you knowingly, willingly step into this role, if you choose to accept it."

Jesse gave Holly an appreciative nod as he lifted a forkful of linguini to his mouth.

"All right, so the plan is to meet back here for Labor Day weekend, when we'll all reveal what we've decided?" asked Becca.

"Yes," said Jesse, his mouth full of pasta. "That's the plan."

After dinner everyone retired fairly early to their rooms, and the house became quiet. As Holly shut the lights off downstairs and walked up to her room, she saw a light peering out of Mo's room. His door was cracked, so she knocked lightly, accidentally pushing the door open. Holly saw Mo on his knees, bent in prayer next to the bed. He hadn't heard her enter, so she silently backed out. She let her hand linger on Mo's closed door as she stood in the hallway, silently asking for God's blessings and peace upon him.

The next morning everyone was up early, and suitcases started filling the front foyer. Holly buzzed about, making sure everyone stopped long enough to eat a good breakfast. As goodbyes and hugs were dispensed, the kids exchanged promises to get together throughout the summer. "Well, if nothing else," said Dave. "We've got Labor Day locked in."

"That's right," Jesse said. "Labor Day weekend we'll do this again. And in the meantime, if you need to talk about this, or anything else for that matter, call me. I am always here for you."

As Holly and Jesse stood outside the front door, waving goodbye to each car as it departed down the driveway, Holly couldn't help but feel a little piece of herself departing too.

CHAPTER 3

EVIE

WATER DROPLETS ROLLED DOWN the floor-to-ceiling windows in the UBU (Urban Bikram Universe) yoga studio in Chicago's posh Lincoln Park neighborhood. The smell of sweat permeated the class filled with nouveau riche women and men all trying to balance their chakras. The humidity pressed hard on Evie as she transitioned from the awkward pose to the eagle pose. Through intense focus and also sheer stubbornness, she willfully accepted her significant physical discomfort and focused on deep, intentional breathing.

"I smell like a hillbilly's trouser legs after he's been chased through a field of skunk cabbage," Addison said with her southern drawl, as she and Evie rolled up their yoga mats after class.

"You can take the lady out of Kentucky, but she won't leave her moonshine metaphors behind." Evie smirked, clearly amused by her friend. "Here, try this," Evie said as she sprayed a few pumps of rose-scented rehydration mist on Addison's face. "It'll make you feel better. It's what we use north of the Mason-Dixon line."

Addison and Evie left the gym, walking along Belden Avenue toward their favorite juice bar, Squeez. "Addie, do you ever wonder why God put you here on earth?" Evie asked.

"Wow, that's intense, Evie," Addison responded. "Are you having an existential crisis? Or are you just trying really hard to make friendly conversation with a southern preacher's daughter? You know I'm here for you either way, sister."

The women ordered their acai smoothie bowls and nabbed a table. As the two friends settled in, Evie gazed through the window, drumming her fingers on the table. "Addie, I think I'm just trying to make sense of my life . . . what it's been, what it is, and what it's going to be. I know I always act like I've got everything together," she divulged. "I know I can roll hot. And that I can be a little cocky. I actually don't like that about myself. In fact, there's a lot I don't like about myself. I mean, my marriage was a total, utter failure. I can be shallow and super self-absorbed," she muttered. "Actually, I'm pretty sure I'm not a nice person."

Addison leaned forward, poised to speak.

Evie put her hand up, motioning for Addison to wait. "Yes, yes, I know there are a lot of good traits that I have too. I'm smart, I'm decisive, I'm a great leader. I kill it at work," she rattled off, flatly. "I think I'm just starting to question what that will yield in the long run. So what, I'll end up in a nice penthouse with a doorman and maybe a role on the board of directors at my company, but I'll be alone, with nothing much to show for it on my balance sheet of life other than financial assets. Shouldn't I be wanting more than that? If I'm as smart as I think I am, shouldn't I be seeking something more fulfilling and meaningful? I mean, why in God's name am I here?" Evie exclaimed, frustrated, as she motioned with her arm toward the sidewalk beyond.

The server placed the two breakfast bowls on the table. "Is there anything else I can get you?" she asked.

"No, thank you kindly," Addison soothed. "We're happy as diamonds in a rhinestone world."

The server tilted her head and paused.

"We're great here, thanks," said Evie, with a slight air of dismissiveness.

"All right, my friend, I think it's my turn to speak here," said Addison. "I'll start off by assuring you that God doesn't make mistakes. *You*," Addison emphasized, pointing at Evie, "you, my girl, are no mistake. I know that to the core of my soul. And even if you don't have all the answers about why you're here, God does."

"Is He going to let me in on it at some point?" Evie asked with a sigh, twirling her spoon through purple puree. "Ugh, why am I feeling this way, Addie?" Evie moaned. "This isn't like me. I don't do this. I'm not reflective and angsty."

"Well," Addison considered. "Did something happen last weekend at your daddy's place that's making you wonder if you're sittin' on a dry waterslide?"

Evie exhaled and put a huge spoonful of smoothie, chopped fruit, and nuts in her mouth. She chewed thoughtfully, licked her lips, and said, "Yes, my dad had all us kids come home so he could invite us to join the family business. He wants us to help him expand Jesse's Hardware."

"Well, I would have thought y'all would be tickled

pink. Your daddy's business has quite the reputation for doing good in the world. I mean, back home everyone knows Jesse's is more than just a place to get a hammer and nails. It's a family that builds up other families. It's a community that serves other communities. And I don't know anyone who could bring more energy and drive to the business than you, Evie," Addison affirmed. "You have a way of making things happen."

"I know, Addie," Evie said. "But Dad's invitation is really forcing me to take a hard look at things . . . like what I want my legacy to be. Prior to last weekend, I was happy with my life here in Chicago, and I would never have considered changing things. But now I'm thinking, Am I truly happy? Or have I just bought into some grand lie about what happiness looks like?"

"Evie, if there's one thing I know about you, it's that you won't let sleeping dogs lie. I know you'll get to the bottom of this and figure out what really cranks your tractor." Addison stood up, grabbing her empty bowl and giving the table a quick wipe with her napkin. "You are here for a reason, Evie. Maybe you should start asking God to reveal your purpose."

Evie nodded silently.

"All right, we should be fixin' to go," Addie said,

leaning over the table to touch Evie's arm. The two friends walked quietly toward their condo complex, both lost in thought but comfortable in the silence.

That night, Evie wrapped herself in a huge faux-fur blanket and cuddled up in the window seat of her fourth-floor condo overlooking Lincoln Park. She rested her head against the window and closed her eyes. "Dear Jesus, what is going on with me? Why am I feeling so unsettled?" Evie asked. "When I was at Dad's house, I told everyone I didn't have to think about it . . . that I knew I could take Jesse's Hardware to the next level. But if I'm honest, that was my big fat ego talking. And now that I'm home, back in Chicago, I'm not so sure I can give up what I have here. I mean, how could I tell my coworkers and friends that I'm leaving my posh agency life to work for my dad's hardware store? They'll think I've lost my mind. But at the same time, I can hear Holly's voice telling us kids that Dad wants this to be our choice—*our* choice. It shouldn't matter what my coworkers think, or my boss, or my friends." Evie exhaled heavily. "Why do I care so much what other people think about me, rather than walking toward You and Your plan for me? When did I stop listening for Your voice? When did I start directing my own path?"

Evie opened her eyes and gazed out the window, instinctively knowing the answer to her questions. Since she had been a teenager, she was never really able to fully put her fate—and faith—in God. It's not as if she questioned His existence or felt comfortable disappointing Him. But she had always felt sure that her plan was the best plan; that she was smart and strong enough to figure her life out. She was self-motivated and self-disciplined, so she would be self-made. *That's a lot of "self,"* she thought. *It's no wonder I can be so selfish.*

Yes, she had handcrafted a life that was almost completely self-directed, in pursuit of things the world said were important. But now she was at a juncture, and she had to decide: Would she stay the course, living luxuriously and enjoying the fruits of an enviable existence? Or would she leave it all behind to join the family business and work in pursuit of something bigger and more personal—something that transcended her own wants and needs to help advance the mission of her family?

Changing her life would involve risk. But one thing Evie was not was risk averse.

After brushing her teeth and going through her nighttime skin routine, Evie knelt down parallel to her bed, easing herself into an extended child pose. She inhaled deeply through her nose and then exhaled, relaxing her diaphragm. After a few minutes, she elevated her head, feeling calmer. Before standing upright, while still on her knees, she scooted over to the edge of her bed and rested her elbows on the plush, organic quilt, bowing her head.

"Jesus, I don't have all the answers. I don't. I need Your guidance to help me choose the right path moving forward. In the days ahead, please guide me. And please help me turn to You for leadership and direction, rather than taking charge myself. I'm not so sure anymore that the path I've chosen so far has been the right one."

Evie's job was intense that summer. Her agency was awarded a number of high-profile, international accounts, and her elite airline status could prove it. She traversed the world in a first-class seat, enjoying projects in London, Berlin, Dubai, Tokyo, and Madrid. When she was home in Chicago, it was only long enough to get her clothes dry-cleaned. Still, Evie managed to go on dates that summer, with the hopes of meeting a nice guy and maybe even a husband. Her dates usually went like this:

"Brad, tell me why a guy like you is still single," Evie would say coyly, tapping her fingers on her chin.

"I just haven't met the right woman yet," Brad would respond, with a slow smile, equally masterfully.

As dinner would progress, Evie would notice how much Brad talked about himself. There would be no banter, no back-and-forth. It would be all one-sided, all about Brad's big job in finance, Brad's new BMW, Brad's stock options. Brad would also—intentionally or not—fiddle with his cufflinks and adjust his Rolex throughout the evening.

This pattern repeated throughout the summer months. There was Oliver in London, Alexander in Dubai, and Daniel in Madrid. Evie never let things go beyond one or two dinner dates because each time, invariably, she would discover at least one major red flag—one she couldn't possibly ignore. What little hope she carried would be instantly dashed. Under normal circumstances, she probably would have enjoyed the company of these men. But something had changed in Evie.

As she jetted from city to city, meeting to meeting, and date to date, Evie's thoughts periodically wandered back to her ex-husband, Andrew. When she really thought about him, stripping away the arguments, the frustrations, and the disappointments, she knew he was a good man. Of course, he wasn't perfect, but he was strong, stable, and caring. In fact, when Evie really thought about the character traits she was seeking in her next partner, she realized Andrew had them.

After a particularly grueling schedule in Japan at the end of August, Evie rushed through Narita International Airport, desperate to make her nonstop flight back home. She was exhausted and feeling unusually fragile. As she ran to make it to her gate in time, she tripped, breaking off a heel and sending her phone and purse careening through the crowd. Evie cursed loudly as she landed on the ground with a hard thud.

Instantly and palpably, the mood around Evie quieted, as the notoriously polite Japanese travelers attempted to ignore her vulgar outburst. Normally, Evie would have been able to dust off an incident like this, chalking up her explosion to being tired, or over-worked, or being human. But this time, shame caused her cheeks to flush red as she scrambled to gather her belongings. Once upright again, Evie slowly limped her way toward the gate, her missing heel and resulting lopsided gait an outward representation of what she was feeling inside.

As Evie settled into her first-class seat on the plane, she was struck by a terrible feeling. Her marriage to Andrew had failed not because of him.

It was her.

She was aggressive, impatient, demanding. She was a control freak and thought her good looks could and should excuse even the most unbecoming behavior. She thought she deserved respect and adoration from Andrew, regardless of how she treated him. She thought he should be able to man up and take her outbursts and tirades, while at the same time honoring her like a queen.

Evie sank lower in her chair as she thought about the men she had dated over the summer. They were wholly unattractive to her because they had unsurmountable character flaws. Alexander was clearly a micromanager. Daniel was very self-absorbed. Oliver thought he could do no wrong.

How am I any different? Evie wondered. *These men were literally carbon copies of me, and I wasn't attracted to any of them.*

Somewhere over the Bering Sea, Evie took out her laptop and began writing a letter to God.

God, I can see it now. I can see what You were trying to tell me all along, except I wouldn't listen. My discussion with Addie earlier this summer went nowhere. For the past three months, I've worked hard at growing and nurturing the very life I had been questioning. I buried the thoughts that were born out of my dad's very important and potentially life-transforming question and instead went back to doing what I do best: working my plan and plowing over everyone in my way. I'm so sorry. For someone who thinks she's so smart, I am a really slow learner. I'm still not sure if I should jump ship and invest myself fully in Jesse's Hardware, but I do know now that I won't continue living as I have.

I have this nagging feeling that I've spent my whole life chasing the wrong target. I don't really know what I should be aiming for, but this isn't it. Please guide me and help me make the right decision when I go back to dad's place next weekend. I need Your leadership, God. If it's Your

will that I join Jesse's Hardware full-time, I pray
You'll make it obvious to me.

Back at her condo in Chicago, Evie paced the floor in her kitchen while she waited for the kettle to boil. She poured a cup of tea and hopped up on the counter, grabbing her cell phone. She stared at the screen for a few seconds and then made the call.

"Hi Margie, it's me, Evie. Yes, it's so nice to hear your voice too! It's been awhile . . . yes, I figured Andrew would be in a meeting. No need to interrupt him; can you put me through to his voice mail? Thanks."

Evie closed her eyes, inhaling deeply and exhaling slowly.

"Hi Andrew, it's me. Not who you'd expect, right? Well, I'm calling for a lot of reasons. But I guess I'll start with I'm sorry . . ."

CHAPTER 4

DAVE

It was Saturday morning, and the lyrical, woody sounds of his acoustic guitar floated over the Huron River. Moms pushed strollers, helmeted kids sped along on their bright scooters, and two men played backgammon on a picnic table under the shade of a stately black walnut tree. From Dave's viewpoint, Ann Arbor was about as idyllic as it could ever get.

After earning his undergraduate degree in psychology from the University of Michigan, Dave was so enchanted with Ann Arbor that he stayed there for grad school and ended up starting his practice there too. He had always known he was a "steady as she goes" kind of person, and as he reflected on his life thus far, he chuckled. There he was, sitting on his favorite park bench, playing riffs on his favorite acoustic guitar, and enjoying a cup of his favorite coffee from his favorite coffee shop, Cahoots Café. Altering routines wasn't something that was attractive to Dave; in fact, he avoided it at all costs. That's why he was really struggling with his dad's invitation to join the family business full-time. He loved his dad with his whole heart, but he also felt this was a really big ask. Maybe it was too big.

Dave stood up and extended his chest, gently stretching his back and shoulder muscles. He finished his coffee and threw the cup in the nearby garbage can. He slid his head and right arm through the guitar strap and hopped on his bike for the short ride to work. As he pedaled, Dave realized that this summer—unlike any other—he felt more than the weight of the guitar on his back.

Dave's first client that day was a woman in her sixties who didn't have strong relationships with her adult children and was struggling over past failures as a parent. Next was a man in his thirties who had developed a feeling that everything was futile, life was meaningless, and there was no reason for hope in this world. The rest of the day was much the same . . . one client had been abused as a child and felt she was forever damaged, another was in a loveless marriage, desperate for a way out.

As Dave locked his office door that evening, he reflected on the faces and stories that represented his client list. There was so much pain and sadness in this single small town. He knew he was making a difference as he tried to help people pursue their own paths toward healthy cognitive and behavioral changes, but the reality remained that his client list was always full and his waiting list continued to grow.

That evening, Dave and his band had a gig at The Ark, the local club that was the heartbeat of Ann Arbor's live music scene. They were regulars there, and Dave always looked forward to their performance nights. Playing in his band lit up something from within Dave; it just felt right.

"All right everyone, the band you've been waiting for. Give it up for SlingShot!"

On cue, Dave and his bandmates launched their signature song, "Who Are You?" as the crowd roared. The band took their fans on a lyrical journey as they progressed throughout their first one-hour set. The vibe was emotional and electric, with people swaying, dancing, and singing. The 400-seat venue was large yet intimate, with a low stage that allowed fans to get close to the musicians.

After the band announced a short break, Dave and his friends put down their instruments and walked over to the bar. "Four beers and a ginger ale," the bartender said as he pushed the glasses toward the band.

"Thanks, Gus," Dave said as he grabbed the ginger ale. "Nice set," he added, fist bumping each member of the band. "I like our new adjusted lineup. I think it works. I could feel it in the crowd . . . I didn't feel the energy drop off."

"I agree," nodded Jon, the lead vocalist. "That was a good move. So I think we should run with our second set as planned too. You guys good with that?"

The band members nodded in agreement.

"Hey, Dave," Gus said, sliding a folded piece of paper across the bar. "More fan mail."

Dave smiled sheepishly and ran his fingers through his curly dark hair as he scanned the bar, looking for the author of the message. He unfolded the paper to see a handwritten phone number enveloped by a big heart. He quickly folded it back up and tucked it in his back pocket. Jon elbowed Dave with a chuckle as the two finished their drinks and jumped back onstage for their second set.

As the band packed up their gear after the show, Nate, the drummer, said, "Hey, Dave, have you made any decisions about your dad's offer? Is the SlingShot heartthrob headed to America's heartland?"

Jon grabbed the mic and sang, "Among the local taverns, there'll be a slack in business, 'cause Jesse's offer came before the music and the rent . . ."

Nate threw his head back in laughter, "Dude! The Oak Ridge Boys? Are you gonna start booking gigs for us in Branson?"

The bandmates laughed as they walked together toward the door.

"The jury's still out," Dave said. "I know I have to make a decision soon, but I'm not there yet."

"Well, not to add any pressure, but you do know that we're on to something here, right?" Nate said. "I mean, at a local level, we've made it. All the booking reps in Michigan have us on their short list. If we produce an album, I think we could really go somewhere. Way beyond the mitten, you know?"

Jon interjected, "Yeah, I agree, but Dave, you've

gotta do what's right for you. No pressure from us . . . you know we've got your back whatever you decide, okay?"

Dave nodded appreciatively and the friends parted ways, disappearing into the moonlit streets of downtown Ann Arbor.

✄

The Saturday morning sunshine flooded Dave's cheerful front porch as he swayed gently on his swing, playing riffs of his all-time favorite roots rock songs. It was crunch time, and Dave had some thinking to do. Next weekend he would be headed back home to Iowa, to meet with his siblings and tell his dad what he had decided regarding joining the family business.

Deep in thought, Dave looked up at the paint peeling along the outside edges of his porch ceiling. He had bought the turn-of-the-century home in Ann Arbor's historic district shortly after starting his practice. It was a small house but filled with character. It had beautiful crown molding, a built-in buffet in the dining room, and pedestal sinks that were original to the house. Dave refinished the floors and repainted most of the rooms, but that was about the extent of the work that was needed. The house had been built at a time when quality craftsmanship and joinery were expected. Therefore, despite its years, the house was still solid as a rock, and Dave had built a very happy life for himself there.

As Dave strummed his guitar, he looked down fondly at Benji, his faithful Saint Bernard. Benji was stretched out in a shadow on the porch, having found the coolest possible spot to rest. "You're a good boy, Benji," Dave said as he leaned over to scratch Benji's head. The dog looked up, raising his eyebrows and simultaneously releasing a big, thick string of drool. "Ahh, this heat is rough, isn't it, boy? Let's get you back inside where it's cooler."

The two made their way into the air-conditioned house, Benji plonking himself down on his oversize dog bed in the hallway. As Dave grabbed a bagel out of the bread box, he tried to envision what his life would look like in Iowa . . . if he acquiesced and joined the family business. Beyond having to sell his house and close up his practice (a business that represented the very fruits of all his schooling, not to mention the graduate school bills he was still paying off), Dave would also have to give up his band and everything they had worked—and played—so hard to achieve.

Popping the bagel halves in the toaster, he wondered if he had it in him to make such a drastic life change. It would be the ultimate sacrifice of his independence, his freedom, his passions, and his life's work. Refilling his coffee mug, he felt seeds of resentment creep in to his spirit.

Why should he have to give up his life for the family business? Why should Dad's mission trump his own goals and dreams? While Dad and Holly claimed that they wanted this decision to be a personal one, made by each child, and that they would respect each person's decision, wasn't there an inherent guilt trip baked in to any response other than yes?

Dave spread a thick layer of peanut butter and jelly on his toasted bagel and walked over to the kitchen table, balancing his plate, mug, and phone. Before eating, he prayed, "Jesus, I know a lot of the feelings I have going on here come from a desire to play it safe and maintain my independence. I also know that these inclinations can push me toward an inward mindset rather than an outward one. Help me to care deeply about the success of my father's enterprise and how its growth would create a positive ripple effect, impacting untold numbers of families and individuals. Most of all, please guide me toward a decision that allows me to be me while I honor You. Amen."

Benji rubbed his nose against Dave's leg, looking up at him with hope in his eyes. "Oh, you like peanut butter, don't you, boy! Here you go," Dave said as he broke off a piece of his bagel and offered it to Benji. The dog wolfed it down without chewing, a peanut butter–colored puddle of drool forming in the corners of his mouth.

Dave swiped his phone off the table, tapped the screen, and called his friend Jon. "Hey, buddy, can you meet me at Cahoot's? Thirty minutes? Perfect. See you then."

Jon was already sitting at a table when Dave arrived. "I already ordered for us," he said. "You wanted a 120-degree soy, no-foam latte with an extra shot, sugar-free vanilla pump, and caramel drizzle, right?"

Dave laughed at his friend.

"Your Americanos are up, fellas!" the barista hollered from behind the counter.

"Thanks, Michele," Jon said as he tucked a few dollars into the tip jar. He walked back to the table and slid a coffee cup toward Dave. "Here ya go. Unadulterated miracle mud. Now tell me what's on your mind."

"I need a little wisdom," Dave said. "I've gotta figure out what I'm going to do about my dad's business offer, and I'm stuck. I want to say no, but my heart isn't letting me off that easy. I feel tormented."

"Do you mean you'd feel guilty saying no?" Jon inquired.

"Yep, I'm pretty sure I would feel guilty," Dave said.

"Why?" Jon asked. "Don't you deserve to have your own life . . . one that works for you rather than your family's expectations for you?"

"Yes, I do, and that's where the trouble lies," Dave said. "I want my life, and I also want to please my father. But I feel like it's an either/or situation. I'm stuck."

"But who made it that way?" Jon asked. "Did your dad tell you that if you joined the family business, you'd have to give up everything here in Michigan, move to Iowa, and put on a Jesse's Hardware apron?"

Dave gazed thoughtfully at the chic, weathered tin ceiling, rubbing his chin. "No, actually, he didn't."

"Okay, what did he say?" Jon asked.

"Actually, he said he *didn't* want us to give up our lives for the company, but rather he wanted us to bring all of ourselves to it," Dave said reflectively. "At the time, I guess I registered that as sacrificing ourselves for the company. But perhaps that's not what he was saying at all."

"Dave, my friend, in your work life, you are so accepting of the gray spaces and obscurities, which is part of what makes you such a great therapist. But in your own life, sometimes you can be a little black and white," Jon said, "and you know I say that with a whole lotta brotherly love."

He continued, "Maybe your response next weekend isn't as simple as 'yes' or 'no.' Maybe there's a third option . . . a 'yes, and.'"

"So what would my 'and' be?" Dave asked.

"I don't have all the answers," Jon said. "I just know that instead of making this an all-or-nothing proposition, it could be an opportunity for you to retain who you are, leveraging it to play a role in advancing your dad's business."

Dave leaned back in his chair, balancing on the back two legs. "You know what? No matter what everyone else says, you really are a smart dude," he said with a smile. "I knew there was a reason I should let you buy me a coffee this morning."

The two friends paused outside the coffee shop as Dave leaned over to release Benji's leash from the dog hitch. Jon stooped to give Benji a scratch. "What a good boy! You want a cookie?" Jon reached into his pocket to grab a bone-shaped biscuit. "Michele, the barista, has got a soft spot for big, hairy, slobbery dogs. Right, you old dog?" Jon said as he punched Dave lightly in the arm.

"I don't know about that . . . seems like she gave *you* the biscuit, Jon," Dave said.

"Yeah, but the best way to get to a man's heart is through his dog," Jon replied. "Everyone knows that."

CHAPTER 5

ZACH

"Jack, there is no question: We are the agency you need," Zach said, pulling a 6 hybrid from his golf bag. "Our strategies have garnered global awards, our creative team is unmatched, and our data analytics blow everyone else's out of the water." He walked over to his ball, leveled his stance, set his knees, addressed the ball, and ripped it, remaining in his follow-through position as he watched it bounce on the green.

"Right on the dance floor," he said with a smile, adding, "Don't forget, with our social team on your side, the Jaegers brand name will be on the lips of every high-net-worth millennial from Boston to Barcelona. This is our home territory."

"Zach, I appreciate what you're doing here," Jack Jaegers said as he approached the golf cart. "But, Son, you must know why I'm basically handing you this account, with just a game of golf and a steak dinner at Spencer's on your expense account. I know your family. I know your father. You don't need to give me the hard sell, Son. You've got it." Jack paused, tipping his visor at Zach, "Now how 'bout we stick to playin' golf today?"

Zach winced as he slid into the cart. "Thanks, Jack. You won't regret it."

On his drive home from Omaha, Zach called the office. "Jaegers is ours. Yep, nailed it. Let's get all hands on deck Monday. We need to get the whole team up to speed on this one."

Zach turned up Hootie and the Blowfish and set the cruise control at seventy-five as he blazed across the border, back to Des Moines.

The next morning, Zach and his girlfriend, Zoey, strolled through the downtown farmer's market. They sipped iced coffees as they filled up Zoey's cotton satchel with organic kale, Kirby cucumbers, and black raspberries.

"So," Zoey said as she inspected a red pepper, "have you given any more thought to your dad's offer?"

"Yes . . . and no," Zach said. "Yes, I've tried to imagine what it might look like to work for the family business, and at the same time, I haven't invested a ton of brain time because I really don't know what I'd be walking into. I have nothing to compare it to. Dad basically just gave us all an open invitation to join the business, without telling us what we would be doing or what kind of benefits he will offer. I tried bringing it up while I was there over Memorial Day weekend, but he didn't respond. I get the sense that he just wants us to trust him." Zach paused, "Truth is, I do trust him—completely. But I also need to know what I'm signing up for."

"Can both of those statements be simultaneously true?" Zoey asked.

The two walked side by side through an aisle of root vegetables.

"I think you've got to be open to the fact that you may not know all the details, even after—even *if*," she interjected, "you accept the job. Taking an active role in the business means you're no longer just a card-carrying member of the family. You're no longer on the sidelines; you're fully invested. At that point, I would think you'd want to do whatever you can within your power to make the business succeed, regardless of the benefit package."

"That makes this feel less like an exciting job offer and more like a life sentence," Zach said. He kicked a brussels sprout that had fallen off a nearby table and added, "Or an exercise in obedience to my father."

⚒

On Monday morning, the conference room was packed, abuzz with chatter. The company's CMO, Susan, sat at the head of the table, with Zach seated to her right.

"All right, everyone, let's get started," Susan said. "As you likely heard, Zach won the Jaegers account on Friday. Yes, that deserves applause and congratulations," she said over the clapping, as she nodded approvingly at Zach. "It's a marquis account, with estimated billings around $60,000 per month. The purpose of today's meeting is to get everyone up to speed so we can begin developing the Jaegers strategy along with media recommendations, which Zach will present next month. With that, I'll hand it over to Zach."

"Thanks, Susan. Yes, winning Jaegers is a huge coup

for our agency. Jack Jaegers is expecting us to take his clothing brand to the next level. On September 14, we will be meeting with the Jaegers executive team to present our industry research, marketing strategy, proposed media plan, and social plan. We need to identify areas of growth and new segments Jaegers can explore, with the goal of achieving a 10 percent increase in market share by the end of their fiscal year next summer. They have their sights set on aggressive growth, and we are the team that will get them there."

"Zach, what did the Jaegers team say about their previous agency; did you learn why the relationship dissolved?" asked Kara, the project manager.

"We didn't touch on that," Zach replied. "If you want to dig up intel, that would be great."

"Will we be completely rebranding Jaegers, or will our design strategy piggyback on their current creative direction?" questioned Claudia, the creative director.

"Jack kept his wishes close to the vest. I think we should make recommendations at our September meeting," Zach said.

"Sure," Claudia responded, "but it would be nice to have some insight as to whether they are attached or not to the current creative . . ."

Zach flushed slightly, as Rob, the company's media director, interjected, "In terms of a proposed media plan, what's our domestic/international allocation mix?"

"Great question, I will follow up on that," Zach replied, as he felt a bead of sweat roll down his back.

Susan placed both hands on the conference table and began to rise, "Okay, I think we all know what to do. Let's get to it. Have a good day, everyone!"

"Hey, Zach, nice work on the account!" said Ellie, the account manager. "That's a big win."

"Thanks, Ellie!" Zach said over his shoulder as he walked toward the break room. Just outside the door, Zach could hear hushed laughter. He bent over to pretend he was tying his shoe.

"I wish I could be so clueless and still get his salary!"

"I know he's a nice guy, but what does he actually do?"

"I heard he got the account because Jaegers is a fan of his father."

His heart pounding audibly in his ears, Zach quickly stood up and made a beeline toward his office, shutting the door behind him. His face and ears were burning, and he was in a full sweat. Zach had always had a sense people questioned his value at the company, but he had never actually had any proof. Today he heard it from the mouths of his team: He was inept . . . useless. A waste of a corner office.

How could they have known he got Jaegers because of Jesse? Of course, that also meant they probably thought he was keeping his job, too, because of his father—clearly it was not on the strength of his own merit.

Zach was humiliated.

He paced his office floor, trying to figure out how he could save face and restore his dignity. He wasn't a slacker! He did have value. Maybe he didn't have the graduate-level marketing degrees that some members of his team possessed, but he was a very likable person with a knack for winning accounts. He *did* bring important contributions to the company.

But what if it wasn't just Jaegers who handed Zach an account because of Jesse? What if, secretly, all of his account wins could be chalked up to his dad?

Zach fell into his office chair, covering his face with his hands. He felt as if he could sob, but he fought against it, pounding his fist against his desk. He stood up and grabbed his gym towel off the back of his door to wipe his face. Taking deep, measured breaths, he worked to slowly regain his composure.

He sat back down at his desk, opened up his laptop, and began writing Jesse an email.

> Dad, I've been thinking about your offer all summer. I know we're getting together in a couple of weeks to talk about it in person, but I thought I'd get a jump on things to let you know that I've decided to join the family business. I think it would be a great opportunity, and I think I could make some really significant contributions toward your expansion plans. Anyway, we'll talk soon, but I just wanted to let you know my decision now.
>
> Love you,
> Zach

Zach rolled his chair back a few inches and exhaled. He felt a tiny bit better knowing he had a plan moving forward. Leaving the agency and joining his dad's business wouldn't combat the peer voices who thought Zach didn't deserve his lot in life. In fact, it would add fuel to their fire. But it would take care of his current problem, and hopefully over time his dignity would be restored. He'd just have to prove to his father—and his brothers and sisters—that he was a productive, effective member of the team.

Ping! Zach checked his inbox. It was a message from his dad. He caught himself smiling; age definitely didn't stop his dad from responding promptly. Jesse seemed to always be at the helm, 24–7.

Hi Zach, so good to hear from you, Son. I'm pleased to hear you've made a decision, and as you'd expect, it makes me very happy to know you are joining the team. You referenced making "significant contributions." I want to put your mind at ease and let you know that your performance will not be judged by the results you generate. I know that's counterintuitive, Son, but it has worked for me. I want those behind the Jesse's Hardware name to bring their whole selves—their personalities, backgrounds, knowledge, experiences, successes, failures, and heartbreaks—to the work. You see, folks may think we are about hardware, but we're not. We're about help, kindness, service, and relationships. When we connect with customers at an authentic level . . . when we are real and relational . . . our business grows. So as you think about your transition to the family business, remember that I don't measure success like your

**marketing agency does. Jesse's Hardware is different.
I hope you find some freedom and comfort in that.**

**Love you, Son!
Dad**

Zach's throat swelled and his eyes filled up with tears. Somehow his dad knew this was exactly the message he needed to hear today.

Zach pressed the button to talk to his assistant. "Susie?"

"Yes! What do you need, Zach?" Susie asked.

"Can you cancel my afternoon appointments? I'm going to work from home for the rest of the day," Zach stated.

As he pulled out of the parking ramp, Zach wondered what it would look like to work full-time for Jesse's Hardware. What would the hours be like? Would he be on call around the clock? What did his dad mean when he said he wouldn't judge results or outcomes? That idea was so radical to Zach and his everything-must-be-measurable mindset. He couldn't even fathom a world where Key Performance Indicators wouldn't rule his life.

He pulled into a front-row parking spot at Francie's, his favorite bar on the south side of Des Moines. It was filled with wood chairs, wood barstools, wood tables, and wood-paneled walls. As the bartender always said, "The world needs a place with more "woulds" and less "shoulds."

Zach's favorite spot at the bar was open, and he slid onto the stool, tapping two fingers on the worn wooden countertop. The bartender nodded at Zach and grabbed a glass. "Hey, my friend. Haven't seen you since that night you had to call in search and rescue." He slid a tall beer toward Zach. "Was your girlfriend mad she had to come and get you?"

"Nah," Zach said with a boyish smile. "Sometimes I think she likes taking care of me." The bartender shrugged. "Wow, man, you're lucky. I don't hear that a lot."

Zach sipped his beer while he answered emails on his phone and texted with Zoey. He wanted to have dinner with her as soon as possible so they could talk about his decision to join Jesse's Hardware.

As the two texted back and forth, Zach felt simultaneously grateful and guilty. Without a doubt, Zoey was the best thing that had ever happened to him. But what did she see in him?

Zach felt a lump rise in his throat. He squeezed his eyes shut for a moment and swallowed hard. When he and Zoey finally got a chance to talk in person, he was 99.9 percent sure he would not divulge the details about his traumatic morning at work; he didn't think his pride could take it. He didn't want Zoey to look at him with pity in her eyes. He desperately needed her to keep seeing the man he wanted to be.

CHAPTER 6

BECCA

"Come on, Hannah Banana! It's time to go!" Becca hollered up the staircase. She walked back into the kitchen to see her husband, Marty, loading the dishwasher. "No, no, I've got it, Marty," she said, nudging him away with a light hip bump. "You still need to get dressed. We're leaving in ten minutes."

Becca finished loading the dishwasher, then grabbed a dishcloth and gave the countertops and kitchen table a thorough wipe down. She scurried through the main level of the house, folding blankets, straightening cushions, putting toys in baskets, and, in general, making sure everything was in apple-pie order.

Becca could hear Marty's footsteps coming down the stairs before she saw him. With each step, Marty groaned, hitting each tread with a thud. "Becca, quick, come here," he pleaded. "My back is killing me. It's almost like I have a tumor or something."

"Oh my!" Becca said with feigned dread. "A tumor! That sounds horrible! Let me take a look."

Marty reached the landing and took a dramatic, labored step forward. Becca slowly spun Marty around to expose Hannah, clinging to Marty's back.

"Boo!" Hannah squealed.

"Aaaaah!" Becca shrieked, throwing her hands up in the air. "Hannah, you really scared me this time!" she said, winking at Marty.

"We got you, Mom!" Hannah said, chuckling.

"Okay, you nutjobs," Becca said, "it's time to go! Last one to the car is a rotten egg!"

The family was headed to Blank Park Zoo for a special all-day fundraiser, the Beastly Bash. It was an invite-only event for zoo donors, with the goal of raising $500,000 in support of a new traveling Zoo Mobile that would bring educational opportunities to young students in low-income communities. As educators, Marty and Becca were in full support of the initiative.

"Here, Banana," Becca said, reaching over into the back seat to hand Hannah a headband with a fluffy lion's mane attached.

"Oooh!" Hannah exclaimed, putting on the headband. "Roarrrrrr!"

"I might need a nap this afternoon," Marty chuckled. He was twenty years older than Becca, and while the age gap hadn't seemed like much when Becca was a twenty-two-year-old kindergarten teacher dating the charming forty-two-year-old school principal, the difference had started to show in recent years.

Becca patted Marty on the hand reassuringly. "I think we can arrange that."

Once they parked, Becca opened the door to let Hannah out and reached into the back of the vehicle to grab her backpack. "All right, troops, let's do this!" she said.

After collecting their name tags and goody bags from the registration table, the family proceeded to the STEM space, where animal-themed activities and projects awaited the kids.

"Mama, can I go?" Hannah pleaded.

"Sure, honey," Becca said, releasing Hannah's hand. "Dad and I will be right here."

Hannah ran at a full sprint toward a large canvas tent.

"I don't know what I was expecting, but it sure is loud in here, isn't it?" Marty asked.

"Yep, if there's one thing kids aren't, it's quiet," said Becca.

"This is actually kind of nice," Marty said. "We aren't responsible for any of these kids, other than our own. We can just smile and nod today."

"True! It's almost like we have a babysitter, too," Becca said. "Because let's be honest: Hannah won't want much to do with us while we're here."

"Is this a date?" Marty asked, laughing.

"It's as close as we're going to get for now," Becca chuckled.

"Have you talked to your family lately?" Marty asked. "Any news from the empire?"

"No, not really," Becca said. "I've tried reaching out to Zach a few times lately, but his responses are less than enthusiastic. I know I hurt his feelings pretty badly over Memorial Day weekend. I don't know why I was so mean to him. I mean, out of all us kids, I'm the closest with him. I'm worried that I did major damage to our relationship."

"Well, you went into that weekend pretty stressed, if I remember correctly," Marty said. "It was the end of the school year, so the timing of your dad's invitation wasn't ideal. And because you feel so comfortable with Zach, he caught the brunt of it. You know, we often hurt the people we're closest to."

"I know you're right, but that actually makes me feel worse," Becca said. "I know how sensitive Zach is, and the fact that I would go after him like that is pretty shameful."

"Well, you are all getting together for Labor Day weekend, right? Why don't you pull Zach aside and tell him how sorry you are in person?" Marty suggested, reaching out to squeeze Becca's hand.

"I will," Becca responded.

"Mama, look at me!" Hannah shouted. She was wearing a gray face mask with a painted paper towel tube attached, forming an elephant trunk.

"Is that you, Banana? It sounds like you, but it doesn't look like you!" Becca teased.

Hannah ran off to a table filled with animal pelts, where a zoo employee was wearing a brown explorer vest.

"Since we're on the subject of Labor Day weekend,"

Marty continued, "do you have any thoughts about your dad's job offer?"

"Not yet, but I'm leaning toward saying no," Becca said. "I just feel like we've got a good life here in Des Moines, you know? I mean, we are established in our community, and Hannah is happy. Plus, I feel like we've worked really hard to put any sort of drama or public spectacle behind us."

Becca lowered her voice to a near whisper. "Do you remember when we started dating, Marty? Do you remember the horror over a young teacher dating the older principal? Do you remember how it felt knowing people were talking about us behind our backs? It was awful. But we persevered because we were in love and we knew we were meant to be together, and the naysayers finally relented.

"But imagine opening our lives back up to public scrutiny? In my dad's business, that comes with the territory. The way we drive, *what* we drive, every word we say, every move we make will *all* be under the microscope. Once we let it be known we are part of the Jesse's Hardware business, there's no more anonymity. We are forever at the risk of being judged, and even targeted, by those who either wish to see us fail or who want to dull the sheen of the company's reputation by pointing out our personal flaws. I don't think I can take it."

"When you put it that way, it sounds like a no-brainer," Marty said in agreement. "Let's get Hannah and see if she's ready to mosey over to the food trucks. I'm getting hungry."

Later that afternoon, true to form, Marty was on the couch, rattling the shingles with his snoring.

"Dad sounds like a zoo animal," Hannah protested.

"He sure does! Maybe we should have left him there!" Becca said with a smile. She was sitting at the table with the family budget spreadsheet and a calculator. For months, Becca had been hoping to redecorate the living room. But to do so, according to her calculations, she'd need to find approximately $5,000 in a budget where every dollar was already allocated. She scanned the columns, trying to figure out where she could capture funds.

As she moved numbers around, she could see it would require more than just cutting back on groceries for a few months or scaling back on movies. The only two columns standing between Becca and a Better Homes and Gardens living room were the couple's 403(b) plans. If she paused their retirement contributions for six months, a new living room would be hers. She looked out toward the living room area where Marty was sawing logs and envisioned what it could look like with fresh paint, two new sofas, a coffee table, and lamps. She caught herself smiling and then shook her head.

Marty would definitely not be on board with this. Not surprisingly, he was starting to think about his future retirement from the school district. Reducing their collective contributions just so Becca could have her perfect living room was not something Marty would support. She could hear him now: "Becca, I know you want to redecorate the living room, but I also know it wouldn't stop with the living room. I say this from experience. Next it would be the guest bathroom and then Hannah's playroom. It doesn't stop, Becca. And saving for retirement is important . . ."

Becca could feel frustration building inside her. She was a hardworking mother, teacher, and wife. She saved money where she could and did her best to honor the family budget. Her one weakness in life was decorating. Nothing made her happier than a picture-perfect house.

She heard a loud yawn come from the living room, as Marty's head popped up from the couch. "Hey,

Sunshine," he said groggily, giving Becca a military salute with his right hand. "What did I miss? Is our ship still afloat?"

"Everything is fine," Becca said curtly.

"Got it," Marty said, wandering off to the bathroom.

Becca wondered why she felt so aggravated by Marty. He actually hadn't done anything wrong; nonetheless, she was mad at him. She got up and poured a glass of water.

Marty walked into the kitchen and stood behind Becca at the sink, putting his arms around her waist. "Are you okay?" he asked gently.

"Yes, I'm fine, Marty," Becca said coolly. "I'm just annoyed. You know how much I want to redo our living room, but since we are maxing out our retirement contributions, I have nothing to work with."

"But I thought you were on board with that decision," Marty said, turning Becca around. "At least you said you were. Has that changed?"

"Yes, I *was* on board last year," Becca pouted.

"But you're not anymore? Listen, honey, if redoing the living room is that important to you, we can make it happen. How about if I sit down with you and we can look over the budget together," Marty offered.

"No, it's fine," Becca said, dejectedly. "I already did, and there's no category other than retirement that will provide the amount we need. Forget it."

Marty's age and wisdom told him to let it go, and he followed that prompting. "Okay, well, if you change your mind, let me know," he said, giving her shoulders a squeeze before retreating from the kitchen.

Becca grabbed the dish towel from the oven door and held it to her mouth, muffling a scream of frustration.

The next morning, Hannah sat at the breakfast table with the grin of the Cheshire cat. "Mama, do you notice anything different about me?" she asked.

"Hmmm . . . well, your hair looks the same, and I know I've seen that dress before . . . oh wait, have you done something new with your makeup? I haven't seen that shade of lipstick before!" Becca said, grabbing Hannah's face and kissing the cinnamon roll frosting off her lips. Hannah squealed and squirmed, trying to get away.

"Okay, Banana, head to the bathroom and wash your face," Becca said. "It's time for church."

Hannah sat in between Becca and Marty in the pew,

coloring quietly on her lap desk, as the pastor dug into 1 John.

"You might come from a Christian family, you might attend church weekly, you might give regularly, and you might even give your time faithfully by serving on a ministry team. But I ask you, do the rest of your life's actions . . . I mean, the ones that happen behind closed doors with no one else watching . . . do those actions align with your faith too? You see, obeying God is not a pick-and-choose practice. You don't get to do it just when it works for you. It's a full-time, full-life endeavor."

"Mama," Hannah whispered, "look at my elephant."

Becca looked down at Hannah's drawing and nodded approvingly, holding a finger to her lips to remind Hannah to be quiet.

By the time the family returned home after the Sunday morning service, whatever tension had existed between Becca and Marty on Saturday had disappeared.

"Alright, hot dog," Marty said as he ruffled Hannah's hair, "what does Hannah want for lunch?"

"Hey, my name's not hot dog!" Hannah protested.

"Oh, I mean, hey Hannah, how about a hot dog for lunch?" Marty teased.

Becca smiled at Marty admiringly. No, they may not

be living a lavish life, but no one could argue that their little family wasn't living a really happy one.

✗

The next morning, Becca and Hannah were in the car by 7 a.m., headed for Park Hill Elementary, where Becca taught kindergarten and Hannah was in second grade. Marty had left earlier that morning. As the principal, he often had to stay later, too, so driving separately just made sense.

Arriving at school that early meant Hannah would bide time in Becca's classroom, eating her breakfast and playing while she waited for her fellow classmates to arrive at 8:15 a.m. As an only child, Hannah was a master at occupying herself wherever she was. This trait was a saving grace for Becca on school days in particular, because she needed that hour each morning to prepare for the day's activities.

At 8 a.m., Marty decided to swing down to Becca's classroom to give Hannah a piggyback ride to her classroom. As he turned the corner into Becca's office, he heard her talking on the phone, so he tiptoed toward Hannah, motioning for her to be quiet as a mouse.

"Yes, benefits department, please," Becca said into

the phone. "Hi, Carol, this is Becca at Park Hill. Say, I just wanted to find out how hard it would be to hit pause on my 403(b) contributions for a spell." Just then, she turned around in her chair to see Marty. He was bent over, fidgeting with the zipper on Hannah's backpack. Becca could tell he had heard everything.

"Well, hi, Daddy!" Becca whispered brightly, holding her hand over the phone.

"I'm going to take Hannah to her classroom now," Marty said tensely. "Hannah, say goodbye to Mom."

"Bye, Mama!" Hannah said, throwing her arms around Becca's neck. Becca desperately tried to make eye contact with Marty, but he wouldn't look at her.

"Yes, I'm still here, Carol," Becca said into the phone as she watched her two favorite people in the whole world walk out of the classroom together, holding hands.

CHAPTER 7

MO

A MASSIVE VAT OF PUMPKIN CHILI was bubbling on the stove as Mo made a well in the center of his dry ingredients, methodically pouring buttermilk, honey, eggs, and melted butter into the enormous bowl. "Alright, the cornbread will be up in twenty-five minutes, Z," Mo said.

"That's good, because our guests are already starting to line up," Z replied, nodding toward the service window as she refilled condiment bottles.

"What have we got today?" Mo asked. "Any families? Any kids?"

"Looks like a lot of men right now," Z said, looking

out the window. "But you know, the kids will come. They always do."

Mo and Z's mobile food truck business, Squash, was on a mission to combat urban food deserts in the Midwest. Thanks to big crowds and strong local media coverage, in less than a year, Squash became the recipient of a sizable grant from a private foundation. The grant would expand Squash's operations beyond Iowa this fall, with two new food trucks headed for Missouri and two more headed for Nebraska. The foundation had a passion for fighting hunger and had promised additional funding for phase two, which would commence next spring.

Yes, it was clear: Mo and Z made a good team in the kitchen and in life. The two had met at Colorado State University when they were freshmen, and at first they were an unlikely pair. Z had jet-black hair, a nose ring, a lip stud, and a neck tattoo. Mo had shaggy blond hair and was unpierced, inkless, and farm-raised. She was from Portland, Oregon, on a full-ride scholarship in pursuit of an English degree. He was from Ames, Iowa, paying full tuition and unsure what he wanted to study. She was a vegetarian; he had been raised on meat and potatoes. Her parents were divorced; Mo's parents had been married for more than thirty years. Her politics were left-leaning; his politics fell on the right side of the spectrum. On paper, they couldn't have been more different. Yet somehow the two hit it off. It started in the cafeteria. Mo was trying to coax a big glob of mashed potatoes off the serving spoon and onto his plate when a voice behind him said, "Here, let me help." Z took a clean spoon from her tray and scraped the mashed potatoes onto Mo's plate.

"Thanks," Mo said shyly, moving along the line.

"No problem," Z said, spooning sautéed spinach onto her plate. "It looks hideous," she said, "but if you cover it in parmesan cheese, it's not half bad. My name is Z. What's your name?"

"Hey, I'm Mo," he said, turning to face her.

"Want to sit together?" Z asked.

"Sure," Mo said.

The two wandered off to a booth and set down their trays. Little did they know that this dinner in Durrell Dining Center would change their lives forever. Z turned out to be an insightful girl with the kindest heart of anyone Mo knew. She had a strong moral compass and a sensitive spirit for those less fortunate. In fact, as they talked, Mo became increasingly enchanted with her and at the same time, more conscious of his own shortcomings.

Z volunteered at the local VA clinic in Fort Collins, providing patient support services. She transported veterans in wheelchairs, escorting them from their clinic appointments to the lab or physical therapy department and sat with them while they waited for care. Z's love for these heroes ran deep, and she had a passion for listening to their life stories. Her heart broke for their pain and regrets, and she listened with rapt attention as they shared moments of honor and glory.

In contrast, Mo didn't do any volunteering. In fact, until he met Z, he pretty much kept to himself. It wasn't that he didn't want to help people who needed it. In fact, back in high school he once got into a fist-fight defending a kid who was being bullied. He was suspended for a few days, and when he came back to school, kids kept their distance from him. It wasn't the reaction he had expected.

Yes, Mo had a quick temper. And, if he was honest, loving others didn't come easily to him. He had to work at it. But as it turned out, he didn't have to work at loving Z. He just did.

Throughout their college years, Mo and Z sought

freedom and adventure in the foothills of the Rocky Mountains. They went mountain biking, hiking, and skiing. Z gave Mo a pair of binoculars from Goodwill and took him birdwatching at Fossil Creek Reservoir, where she adeptly spied hooded Steller's jays and colorful western tanagers. While they walked, they were quiet—in search of birds, yes, but also in pursuit of something deeper and more meaningful. Z called it connecting with her Maker. Mo didn't know if she was speaking of the same God whom he had been raised to believe in and pray to, but if her life was a manifestation of her faith, he felt sure they were one and the same.

On one of their walks, Mo found a beautiful five-foot-long piece of aspen alongside the trail. He picked it up, only to drop it quickly with a shriek. "A spider almost bit me!" he said, frantically. When he saw Z's face erupt from initial concern into a smile and then full-blown laughter, he couldn't help but laugh too. From then on, Mo carried his aspen walking stick on their journeys. Z said it was his staff to part the sea of spiders.

While he was with Z at CSU, for the first time in his life, Mo felt the walls around his heart begin to crumble. He was happy—really and truly happy.

After graduation, Mo took a job with the food bank

for Larimer County and Z worked for the VA. That fall, they were married in a small outdoor ceremony with just their closest family and friends. Z wore a flowing ivory dress and a wreath of dried Colorado wildflowers that she had carefully pressed earlier that summer. As they said their vows under a vine-covered arch, a light breeze shook the aspen trees, and the leaves quaked with soft applause.

For their honeymoon, the newlyweds jumped into Mo's rusty blue Camry and took off—no reservations, no map. Z just wanted to ride shotgun, enjoying the freedom and excitement of the open road with her best-friend-turned-husband, Mo.

"Mo! Mo! Hey, back to earth! Cornbread's done!" Z hollered as she expertly chopped scallions into a large stainless steel bowl.

"Sorry, on it," Mo said, grabbing two thick towels for oven mitts. As he pulled the sheet pans of cornbread out of the oven, he said, "Man, I've got to get my head in the game! I'm feeling distracted."

Z snapped his backside with a kitchen towel and said, "Well, you're in luck. I'm feeling 100 percent on my game today. Follow my lead." With a grin that never ceased to melt Mo's heart, Z rolled up the service window and shouted, "Hello, friends! Today we are serving our famous Squash chili and cornbread. I hope you're hungry!"

For the next two hours, Z and Mo operated like clockwork in the food truck. Each person received a bowl of chili with sliced scallions and sour cream and a slice of warm cornbread with a dollop of whipped honey butter on top. All of the bowls, plates, and utensils were biodegradable—an expense that Mo and Z felt was nonnegotiable as part of their desire to run an eco-friendly operation. Z made a point of making eye contact with each person who received a meal; this, too, was core to Squash's mission. They wanted each person struggling with food insecurity to be offered a meal *and* human connection. In all, they handed out approximately 200 hot meals that day.

As Mo and Z washed dishes, wiped down appliances, and sanitized their work surfaces, Mo said, "I am completely exhausted. I'm not sure why, but I feel like my butt has been kicked clear across the field. I really need to get some sleep."

"Well, let's get this wrapped up then!" Z said with a smile. "We're almost finished, and then you can sleep like a baby."

Two hours later, Mo was staring at the ceiling, frustrated. His body was yearning for sleep, yet his brain wouldn't cooperate. It was buzzing.

"You awake?" Mo whispered.

Z rolled over and said groggily, "I am now."

"I don't know what to do about my dad's invitation to join the family business. I mean, I really don't want to do it and, if I'm being honest, I am actually kind of mad that he asked. It feels like an infringement on my life—on our life—and everything we've worked so hard to achieve. We are good at what we do, Z. We help a whole lot of people. For my dad to think his operation is more important than ours feels arrogant."

"Hmmmm," Z said softly, "arrogant? That's not a word I would ever associate with your dad. Loving, authoritative, strong, passionate, stable, wise . . . those are words that come to mind when I think about Jesse, not arrogance." Z cleared her throat. "I think his motives are pure, Mo. In my opinion, this was an invitation for you to get closer with him. I believe he views this as an opportunity for your family to unite together as you work toward a shared purpose. He just wants his kids to be a part of his life."

"You're a good person, Z," Mo said with a tinge of

shame in his voice. The two lay in silence. "So where's all this internal anger coming from? Why do I feel this way?" Mo tried to mask the desperation he felt in his gut.

Z rolled on her side and propped her head up to face Mo. "Do you want my honest opinion?" she asked.

"Of course," Mo said slowly.

"When you are afraid or feel like something is out of your control, your instinct is to respond with anger," Z said gently. "I think something about your dad's offer makes you feel afraid."

Mo rolled on his side to look at Z. "That doesn't make sense to me. Why would I be afraid of joining my dad's business?"

"You are a man of plan and purpose, Mo," Z said. "And this job offer was not part of your plan. I think your dad's offer caught you by surprise. And because it involves work that you may not necessarily understand or feel prepared for, your gut reaction is to reject it."

"You're right, it did catch me off guard," Mo said. "I'm not sure why, actually. When I really think about it, the signs were there all along that Dad wanted us kids to join him. We just chose not to take note because it was easier to pursue our own lives. We thought we were flying under his radar."

"Remember when we started Squash last year?" Z asked. "We were a little scared investing in our food truck. It was a big step for us, and we certainly didn't know how it would play out. But we moved forward, risks and all, and put one foot in front of the other each day. We had hopes, for sure, but no real expectations of how Squash would do. We overcame our fear of failure by simply doing it—by showing up. If you choose to really consider this opportunity with your dad's business, you might need to embrace the same approach."

"But what about Squash? I can't leave our business to work with my dad. Squash is basically our first child," Mo said.

"Don't get so far ahead of yourself!" Z chuckled. "You don't need to have everything figured out. You're not in charge of the world, Mo, or responsible for it, either."

She touched Mo's face. "Sometimes when you give up all control, things come together in ways you never could have possibly imagined."

Mo slept peacefully that night for the first time since Memorial Day weekend.

The next week was a whirlwind as Z and Mo prepared for their first big public fundraising event at Greenwood—Ashworth Park in Des Moines. Thanks to their volunteer committee, the benefit was shaping up nicely. It would take the form of an outdoor family festival with carnival games, a silent auction, food from the Squash mobile, and music from Dave's band, SlingShot. Their committee chair, Beth, ran her own event-planning company in town, so Mo and Z had faith their fundraiser was in the best possible hands.

On the eve of the big day, Dave and his band drove in from Michigan. "Mo! Brother! So good to see you!" Dave said as he climbed out of the van, greeting Mo with a hearty embrace.

"Thanks for coming!" Mo said gratefully. "We are so appreciative you guys could make this work with your schedule. We know a small-town nonprofit event like ours can't compete with the gigs you have booked. It means a lot that you would make this happen."

"Of course! This is a great cause, Mo. You're doing important work here," Dave said, slapping Mo on the back.

As Mo led Dave and his bandmates to the backyard, Z opened the sliding glass door and emerged holding a massive tray filled with plates and bowls. "Ah, our headliners have arrived! Welcome, fellas!" Z said, putting down the tray on the patio table. She made the rounds, giving everyone a hug and inviting them to sit around the table.

The bandmates dug into platters of chicken skewers, beef kebabs, roasted vegetables, and warmed pita bread with garlic olive oil. The mood was relaxed, and the little backyard was filled with vibrant conversation and laughter. As the meat platter made the rounds, Z held a kebab in the air, waving it lightly as she said, "See how much I appreciate you guys? I cooked meat for you! Now that's true love . . ."

"For the record, we *are* still paying you too," Mo added with a smile. "But really, we want to thank you all so much for coming this weekend. We're grateful for your support."

"We're family, Mo," Dave said, gesturing around the table. "That's what brothers do. We work together, especially when it's for the greater good."

CHAPTER 8

HOLLY

JESSE STOOD IN THE DOORWAY, watching Holly slowly walk around the dining room table, pausing at each chair long enough to place her hands on it and pray for the child who would be sitting there that evening. Along the way, she straightened napkins and silverware, brushed lint off the tablecloth, and adjusted the glassware. Jesse smiled. Holly truly was love personified. He patted the old oak casing of the doorway softly and appreciatively as he turned, retreating to his study.

When Holly reached the place where Emma used to sit—at the foot of the table, opposite Jesse—she stopped. Her heart yearned for Emma's physical presence this weekend, but of course, that was not possible. Holly prayed that she would be able to somehow bridge the gap left by Emma's absence; that she could help the children clearly see Jesse's heart and intention, so they could make their decisions based on truth, rather than assumptions or misunderstandings. She said aloud, "Emma, I can't guide the children without you. Please help me offer compassionate understanding and wise counsel. Help me encourage them to recognize and use their gifts. And help me to step back, allowing each child to make their own choice, even if they don't fall in line with Jesse's plan."

That evening, it would be just Holly with the kids. Jesse had urgent business to attend to at one of his stores, but he promised to be back on Saturday morning. "It'll be great," Jesse said, reassuring Holly. "Over the years, you've always done such a beautiful job filling in for me and Emma with the kids. You know what to do."

The atmosphere in the living room that evening was palpable to Holly. Everyone was chatting and laughing, seemingly having a good time, yet she could feel an undercurrent of tension, or perhaps it was apprehension. Each child appeared to have a weight on his or her shoulders—one that was uniquely theirs, yet collectively, it rested heavily on the family.

"Hey, Zach, come here a second," Becca said, motioning for Zach to follow her into the kitchen. Becca leaned back against the kitchen island and crossed her arms.

"Uh-oh," Zach said, "what did I do?"

"Oh! No," Becca said, uncrossing her arms. "It's not you, Zach. It's me. I know I really screwed up when we were all together over Memorial Day weekend. I don't know why I was so mean to you! I am so very sorry. Do you hate me?"

"Of course I don't hate you, Becca!" Zach said. "You're my little buddy!"

"I know I am," Becca said. "Marty thinks you were the target of my wrath because out of everyone, I'm most comfortable with you."

"Ah," Zach nodded.

"So with that logic, I guess that makes you lucky?" Becca suggested with a big smile, throwing her hands up in the air.

"Yep, I'm lucky, all right," Zach said as the two walked arm-in-arm back to the living room.

Standing silently in the butler's pantry, Holly wiped a tear of gratitude from her cheek.

When the meal was ready, following Holly's prompting, the children took their seats at the dinner table. "Your father is so sorry he can't be here," Holly said, "but he knew you would understand. He'll be back tomorrow. Becca, could you please bless our meal?"

"Sure, Miss H," Becca said. "Thank you, Lord, for all thy many blessings. Amen."

"I feel like I know that prayer. Becca, don't you have that framed in your kitchen?" Evie asked wryly. "Did you give us a canned, cross-stitch prayer?"

Becca stuck her tongue out at Evie, then cooed, "Oooh, I love your mashed potatoes, Miss H!" as the bowl was passed around.

"Yeah, Miss H," Zach added, "it looks like you've got all your greatest hits here! Prime rib? Homemade macaroni and cheese? There's enough food here for all of Ames. It's a feast!" Then Zach cleared his throat and feigned concern. "Uh-oh, which one of us is the prodigal son?"

Becca laughed, perhaps a little too loudly.

"It's not just one of the boys who could be lost," Evie said quietly, taking a sip of her wine.

Any illusion that this gathering was simply a social one had just been put to rest. *The subject of the day has officially been broached*, Holly thought as she silently refilled water glasses. *And so it begins.*

"Evie, what are you talking about?" Becca asked. "Out of all of us, you've always been the überachiever, the doer, on track to reach your goals. I'm not sure I can think of an opportunity you've ever squandered."

"Let me help you, Becca," Evie said. "I've squandered my marriage, my purpose, my values . . ." her voice trailed off for a moment. "I could go on. This summer was one of personal reckoning for me, and to be honest, I didn't like what I saw. It started off as an innocent inquiry into my reason for being, and it ended up exploding into an existential crisis."

"Whoa, Evie, that sounds really intense," Dave said sympathetically. "What do you think is at the root of your inner turmoil?"

Mo looked appreciatively at Dave, grateful for his brother's sensitivity and experience navigating these types of conversations.

"Well, this summer I realized I'm an ugly person. I know this probably does not come as a surprise to you all, but I am ego-driven, prideful, and controlling. I pursue all the wrong things for all the wrong reasons, and in the meantime, I seem to have a knack for pushing away anything that's truly good." She paused. "Over the past three months, I've realized the true depths of my shortcomings and failures."

The table fell silent for what felt like minutes. Holly got up to retrieve a dish from the sideboard, and as she returned to the table, she walked past Evie, touching her shoulder softly.

"Well, if it makes you feel any better, I had a rough time this summer too," Mo offered. "In fact, I'm not sure I could have processed it without Z. She helped me realize that I also have control issues," he said, nodding toward Evie. "It must be a family trait. But mine manifests itself as anger. When I'm uncomfortable or faced with a situation where I'm not in control, I get defensive and explosive. Instead of facing into it, I want to flip the board and walk away."

Holly offered the bread basket to Zach.

Zach picked up a roll and said, "So have you guys made your decision yet about joining the business? Because I have. I emailed Dad a few weeks ago to tell him I'm in."

"Really? That's it? It sounds like it was an easy decision for you, Zach," Evie said. "You didn't experience any painful soul-searching? No mental gymnastics?"

Zach shifted in his seat uncomfortably as he broke his bread roll into two halves. "Well, I wouldn't say it didn't come without discomfort. But yeah, I made the decision pretty quickly."

"Well, I think I've made my decision too," Dave said, adding, "but it sure wasn't an easy one. I really struggled over the idea of making such a huge life change and giving up everything I have going in Ann Arbor. But thanks to some sage advice from my friend Jon, I think I'm going to talk with Dad about it. I want to join the business with my whole life, which means my therapy practice, and my band, and my dog . . . it's all part of me, so it all comes with me."

"What does that look like, Dave? I can't even begin to see how you could blend those two worlds," Becca said, chewing slowly.

"Well, I'll have to discuss it with Dad, but my initial thought was I could work remotely, from Michigan, and be in charge of administering a new mental health benefit for company employees. Quality mental health care and early interventions are vital for people who are struggling. I see it in my practice every day, and on a personal level," he added, "it sounds like a few of us could have used some professional support ourselves this summer."

Becca's face lit up. "I love that, Dave. I never even thought of that as an option. Why should we try to squeeze ourselves into a mold within the business when we could potentially create new roles that haven't been defined yet? Or better yet, blend it all together! Roles that not only draw from our own unique skills and experiences, but build upon them? That's *so* smart," she said admiringly.

"Well, although this past summer exhausted me," Evie continued, "and forced me to face some really uncomfortable truths, I made a decision as well. I'm leaving Chicago behind and moving to Ames to join the business. I think I need a hard reset on my life, and I just don't think I can do it in Chicago. I'll be too tempted to fall back into my old patterns."

"Have you given any thought to what your role might look like?" Mo asked.

"Well, yes, I did," Evie said. "And then I stopped myself. Asserting control and dominating others is what has gotten me into the emotional jam I'm in now. I know I can bring some finances to help the business expand in new places, and there are some locations where Dad has wanted to expand for a long time, but if I'm really committing to a new life, that means I've got to give up my old ways. I'm going to talk with Dad about my role and see what he thinks is best. I don't trust myself right now; I really need to lean on him for guidance."

"That sounds wise, Evie," Mo said. "At least you know Dad will have your best interest at heart. He won't steer you wrong."

"For the record, I'm in too," Mo added. "I'm not exactly sure what my role will look like, but I'm willing to be open to what Dad has in store for me and give it my best shot."

Dave elbowed Mo gently and said, "Way to go, brother. That's a big step for you."

"Yeah, it is! Actually, it's a big stretch," Mo said. "Just ask Z. She's been telling me for a long time that the world will keep spinning, regardless of what I do. So I can either continue to live in fear about everything that's out of my control and angrily try to assert my control over it, or I can try to relax my expectations, which are often unrealistic, and trust that things will work out as they're supposed to. I'm not in charge of keeping the earth on its axis."

"Thanks, Miss H," Zach said as Holly refilled his glass. He took a sip and closed his eyes for a moment, only to open them slowly and look up at the ceiling.

"Geez, everyone is being so open and honest here tonight. I'm not going to be the jerk who pretends like he's got his life all pulled together." Zach cleared his throat, "Guys, I've got a confession to make. My decision to join the company was not as easy as I made it out to be. In fact, I was kind of forced into it. There was a situation at work, and I was completely humiliated . . ." Zach's voice cracked. He closed his eyes again, inhaled deeply and continued, "And if that hadn't happened, I'm not sure I would have agreed to join the company. But it did. And I am. I'm just hoping that even though I may have initially said yes because I was running away from my mess of a life, I can be a strong team player in support of Jesse's Hardware."

The siblings all rallied around Zach. "Aw, Zachie, come here," Evie said, pulling Zach toward her for a side hug that lasted longer than either of them expected it to. The others supported Zach with nods and words of affirmation.

Ever the therapist, Dave asked, "If our parents were

sitting here at the table with us tonight, what do you think they'd say to you, Zach?"

Zach shook his head, unable to answer.

"I think they would tell you they love you, they are proud of your honesty, and they are so happy to hear you are stepping forward. It's as simple as that."

Holly looked across the table and stared intently into Zach's eyes, the warmth of her smile soothing his spirit.

Zach nodded appreciatively, his cheeks still flushed. "I hope so. I want to turn my shame and embarrassment into something that can be used for good. I really do want to help make a difference in expanding the family business."

"It appears we all do, in one way or another," Mo said.

"Not so fast—we haven't heard from Becca yet," Evie said.

"I guess I'm going to put the toilet in what otherwise would have been a royal flush," Becca said, shrugging. "As per usual, I'm going to be the odd man out here. Guys, this won't work for me right now on a number of levels. Hannah is settled in her school, and for that matter, Marty and I are too. We have a nice, quiet life in

Des Moines. And even if we were able to stay there, I'm just not interested in having the kind of scrutiny that comes from being part of the Jesse's Hardware team. Nowadays, people are so aggressive and quick to point out everything they disagree with or can find fault in. If for some reason they have a problem with our family's business, then they have a problem with each of us, too. I just can't take that kind of ongoing pressure and exposure."

"Becca, if I can play devil's advocate for a minute," Evie said, "don't people already know you are part of the Jesse's Hardware family? I'm not sure how joining the business in an official capacity will change that."

"Actually, very few people know I am a part of this family," Becca said. "I mean, our friends from church know, and my childhood and college friends. But for the most part, in my adult life, I've gotten pretty good at hiding Jesse's Hardware and my association with it from the world. I never talk about it, I don't include any references to our family in my work or social circles, and I avoid discussing it with my neighbors. I know it sounds selfish when I say it out loud, but it's for my family's self-preservation. Marty and I really like living in anonymity."

"That seems like the attitude of someone who is ashamed. Are you ashamed of your family, Becca?" Dave asked earnestly.

"No, not at all," Becca said. "I'm not ashamed of you guys, but I also don't feel the need to talk about the family with everyone I meet. What if someone doesn't like Jesse's Hardware or had a bad experience with one of our employees? Then I'm automatically lumped in with that negativity too. What if I start talking about the family and people think I have a big head or a superiority complex? Yeah, there are a lot of different ways a conversation about our family could go south, and I'm not interested in any of them. I'd rather just keep my mouth shut."

"Okay, let me ask you this," Zach said, rubbing his chin. "Let's pretend a neighbor down the street is watering his lawn. You walk by with Hannah and you guys strike up a conversation. He tells you about a really hard house project he's been working on, one where he's stuck and doesn't know what to do next. He's actually pretty frustrated about it. Now you, as a member of the Jesse's Hardware family, know that there's a tool that can help him solve that vexing problem. It's not a complicated tool, and it'll almost certainly complete the project, not to mention restore peace in his household. Do you tell him about it? Or do you keep quiet?"

"Honestly, I wouldn't tell him," Becca said. "I've been down that road before, Zach. It doesn't stop with the tool suggestion. Then they want to know how to use it, they want to talk about getting more tools, they tell other people that I have an 'in' with Jesse's Hardware. Then people start looking at my house and I hear them whispering around town, wondering why I haven't fixed this or patched that when I have access to the world's best hardware store. No matter how hard I try in that scenario, I always end up either being the neighborhood know-it-all or the person who doesn't practice what she preaches."

"Time for a reality check, guys. Let's not pretend that we don't all do this to some extent, at one time or another," Evie said. "Anyone who says they brandish the family name freely, at all times, is not telling the truth."

"You're right," Mo said. "As much as I hate to admit it, I pick and choose the times I play the family card. When I do, I know I'm taking a risk, because I'm casting myself as a representative of us all. That means expectations are elevated and, right or wrong, there's a certain standard I have to live up to." He paused. "So in my case, if I lose my temper with a lazy food vendor or an annoying member of our local government in Des Moines—even if I believe I'm justified—there's a risk I will have tarnished the family name, perhaps forever, for that person as well as their family and friends. That's a lot of pressure, and I'm not sure it's worth it. So I reserve sharing my family affiliation for circumstances I deem to be 'safe,'" he said, raising his hands to make air quotes. "Bottom line is, you're not alone, Becca."

After the dinner dishes were finished and the kids were all together relaxing in the living room, Holly climbed the stairs to her writing attic. She opened the windows, the late summer breeze ushering in the scent of Russian sage as the rhythmic call and response of the katydids filled the air with song. She sat down in her chair and began to write. Her hand moved swiftly, effortlessly, across each page as she documented her deepest thoughts and observations. She wrote passionately and thoughtfully, joyfully and tearfully. Hours passed, and by the time Holly was finished, the house was silent. All the children had gone to sleep.

CHAPTER 9

JESSE

The next morning, Jesse sat at the head of the dining room table, drinking his coffee and reading from a neat pile of documents stacked before him.

"Morning, Dad!" Dave said, taking a seat next to his father. "How was your trip? Everything go okay?" he inquired, pouring himself a cup of coffee.

"Dave! Good morning, my son! Yes, yes, everything is fine. There was a situation that I felt would best be resolved if I made an appearance."

"Sometimes a visit from the CEO is all it takes to make things right again," Dave agreed. "Hey, Dad, before the others come down for breakfast, do you mind if I talk with you about something?"

"Sure, Dave, what is it?" Jesse asked.

"Well, I'm not sure if Holly told you, but last night we all shared our decisions about joining the family business. I told everyone that I want to join you, but I also don't want to give up the core elements of who I am."

Jesse nodded and said gently, "Tell me who you are, Dave."

Dave leaned back in his chair. "I'm a therapist, I'm a musician, I'm creative, I'm reliable, I'm a free spirit, and I'm also a homebody. I love Michigan, I love my life, and I love you," he said, pausing, "and I'm just trying to figure out how to make all of that come together into one job description."

Jesse sat back, a look of deep satisfaction on his face. "Ahhh, Dave, I love you so much. You are honest and earnest, passionate and purposeful. Holly told me you had an idea of how you might pour this life you love into Jesse's Hardware, and I couldn't be happier. As I said back in May, I don't want you to change who you are for the business. I want you to bring everything you've got to it."

"So you'd be open to me sharing some ideas?" Dave asked.

"Of course!" Jesse said. "I can't grow this business without you."

"Thanks, Dad," Dave said, noticing he felt slightly emboldened and empowered.

One by one, the other kids joined the family at the breakfast table, each one greeting their father, and each one, eventually, sharing their decision with him.

"Well, Evie and Mo," Jesse said, reflecting on the thoughts and feelings his children shared, "it sounds like you two are asking for my guidance as you step into the business."

"Yes, as your two kids who are control freaks, we're making an effort to take our hands off the wheel," Evie said.

Jesse linked his hands behind his head and leaned back in his chair. "Hmmm, well, that really opens things up a lot. There are actually very few people like you two—people who are willing to do whatever is required at any given time. If you are open to *anything* . . ." Jesse's voice trailed off, as he was deep in thought.

"When you say 'anything' like that, it feels a little unnerving," Evie said, pretending to bite her nails anxiously.

Mo smiled and said, "Yeah, Dad, to be honest, I

don't know that we are open to *anything*. Maybe it's more accurate to say that we're open to hearing what you think would be best for us."

"And then you can decide how you feel about my suggestions?" Jesse asked amiably.

"Yes!" Evie said quickly, only to stop herself and say sheepishly, "Whoa, I guess control freak recovery takes a little longer than I thought."

Mo laughed and added, "Yeah. Giving Dad the authority to make decisions while reserving the right for ourselves to have the final say is definitely not relinquishing control."

Jesse chuckled. "Rome wasn't built in a day, you two. Making a big life transition like this is not going to be neat and clean. It's bound to stir up some questions and discomfort . . . it will really stretch you. I'll tell you what: How about I keep thinking of roles that I feel would match your personalities and experiences, and you can let me know how you feel. It'll be an ongoing conversation. How does that sound?"

Evie and Mo nodded in agreement.

"Okay, Zach, how about you? How can I help you move into your new role?"

"What new role?" Zach asked. "I have no idea what you want me to do."

"Well, how about if we start with a simple question: If I were to talk with your coworkers or your closest friends, what would they tell me about you?"

Zach's face fell, his cheeks flushing with the humiliation that had taken residence in his spirit over the summer.

Holly caught Zach's eye and said, "Zach is a trustworthy, honorable man and a genuine soul."

Evie jumped in, "Zach is a sales phenom. There's not a deal he can't close."

"No one has a better sense of humor than Zach," Becca chimed in, flashing a bright smile at her big brother. "He's hilarious!"

Dave added, "Zach has the kind of personality that brings people to the table. He's magnetic."

"Zach has a tender heart, and people can sense that. It's why he's always had way more friends than me," Mo added with a little smile.

Zach's lower lip quivered as he fought back tears.

"Zach, my boy," Jesse said gently. "Whatever lies you've allowed to seep into your heart, I want you to reject them. Even if you can't see clearly right now, your family can see for you. Your brothers and sisters see the real you . . . *I* see the real you." Jesse paused. "You are loved more deeply, more purely, than you will ever know. You are a good man with good intentions. I couldn't be more honored to have you step into what will surely be the most important role of your life."

Zach smiled appreciatively as a tear rolled down his face. He slowly, carefully rolled up one of his shirt sleeves, revealing his forearm. "I got this tattoo a few weeks ago. I never thought I was the tattoo type, but for some reason it just made sense to me."

On Zach's arm, in neat black printing, it said:

Then I heard the voice of the Lord saying,
"Whom shall I send? And who will go for us?"
And I said, "Here am I. Send me!"

ISAIAH 6:8

"I want you to use me as you see fit, Dad," Zach said. "I'm ready."

"Come here, Son," Jesse said, as he stood up and invited Zach toward him. When Zach was within arm's reach, Jesse pulled him in for a hug stronger than anything Zach had experienced before. Jesse's arms were shields that offered Zach shelter from the pain of the world, while at the same time fortifying his spirit with an untold source of strength. Zach felt a spark of renewal flicker within him.

As the two returned to their seats, Jesse was clearly moved. "You kids," he started, clearing his throat, "you kids mean the world to me. Bring your worries to me. Bring me your pain. I am here for you . . . to share the burden with you. You don't need to go through life alone. I am here for you always. Lean on me."

Holly floated around the table, quietly refilling coffee cups, which gave her the chance to stop at each chair and lay a hand on each child's shoulder.

"Miss H?" asked Becca. "Could I have a poached egg?"

"Sure, it'll just take a few minutes," Holly said, retreating to the kitchen.

Mo looked at Becca quizzically. Becca responded with a shrug.

"Kids, how about if you get the horses ready for our ride this morning," Jesse suggested. "I'll wait here with Becca."

Once the others were gone, Jesse said, "Becca, you're the last one! We didn't get the chance to fully discuss your decision." He stirred his coffee thoughtfully. "I understand your concerns about being part of this family, or rather, your hesitancy to talk about being part of this family. You're right, our family is not perfect, and that opens all of us up to public scrutiny. I can see how it would be easier to hide your association with us altogether." Jesse placed his elbows on the table and leaned forward. "But what if you could play a role in changing the way people see us?"

"I'm not following . . ." Becca said.

"Well, making sure each member of our family consistently behaves with grace, maturity, humility, and honesty would be an impossible task, right? No human could do that." Jesse paused. "So instead of wishing we were all perfect, or hiding your family membership from others, what if you focused on correcting your own behavior?"

Becca's eyes widened and her cheeks burned. "What do you mean?" she asked, her voice tinged with shame.

"As you know, there are plenty of people who think the Jesse's Hardware family must all walk on water," Jesse said. "But that's never been the case. Struggling and falling down is part of the journey." Jesse reached out and placed his hand over Becca's. "One of the things

I've always tried to encourage in you kids is to own your mistakes and flaws, learn from them, and use them to do better next time. I've never told you to hide them."

Becca felt confused, and at the same time, exposed.

"Think of it this way," Jesse continued. "The most frantic customers we get at the store are the ones who have an urgent need, right? Something is broken, and they need the right tool to fix it right away. After they fix the problem, they often feel a sense of relief and maybe a sense of accomplishment, too. Some even talk about the fix with their friends and family because they are excited they found a solution. That's how we grow. Now new people who are having similar problems know where to look for help." Jessed leaned back. "You may not want to help grow the family business right now, but let me encourage you to at least consider not being afraid to admit you are part of our family, Becca. Even if you struggle and fall. The goal is not perfection. The goal is progress. You don't need to hide your mistakes. Jesse's Hardware has always been built on genuine relationships, and relationships grow in transparency."

"Dad, I'm really confused here. I don't know where this is coming from," Becca said.

"Becca, why did you ask Miss H to make you a poached egg?" Jesse asked tenderly.

"Because I wanted one," Becca said slowly.

"I think you wanted her to leave so she wouldn't be part of our conversation," Jesse said.

"Why would I do that?" Becca protested.

"You know how close Holly was with your mother—they were inseparable. A thought would enter your mom's mind and exit Holly's mouth. Now that your mom is gone, Holly is the closest thing you have to your mom's audible voice," Jesse said. "Do you remember what your mom said each morning when we'd open the store together?"

Becca sighed happily. "Listen, love, smile, and share. Today's the day we show we care."

"That's right," Jesse said. "You didn't think she was only talking about the customers, did you?"

Just then, Miss H walked in with Becca's poached egg. "Here you go, my beautiful girl," Miss H said, as she ran her fingers lightly through Becca's hair.

Becca pushed her chair back and turned, hiding her face in Holly's neck as she did when she was a child.

"There, there. I know," Holly said, consoling her as Jesse quietly straightened the stack of papers before him.

He secured them with a white grosgrain ribbon and placed them on Holly's silver tray, ready to be returned to her writing attic upstairs.

Later that evening, Jesse sat on his Adirondack chair, gazing out at the rolling hills. Dazzling streaks of pink, orange, and red filled the night sky. Holly touched Jesse's shoulder as she approached. "Tea?" she asked, offering him a mug. He accepted it with a smile and a nod as Holly sat down next to him.

"My heart is full, Jesse," Holly said tenderly. "The children are gifts. Each one is so special."

She paused, watching the vivid watercolors fade to midnight blue along the horizon. "How do you think today went?"

Jesse smiled. "It was good."

Afterword

WHEN WE SAID YES to following Jesus, we joined His family of disciples.

The roots of our family go deep—more than two thousand years. They go back to His ascension, when Christ passed the torch to all of us who follow Him (Acts 1:8). This rich family legacy, and the mission Jesus passed on to us, should be a source of comfort and reassurance to us all.

Yet many of us go through life wondering what our true purpose is. We often feel lost or aimless or dissatisfied because we don't know why we've been put on this earth. Some of us think our life's dots will be connected when we finally receive our calling from God.

But the truth is, the call has already been made. The offer is on the table! As members of God's family, we've all received the invitation to pursue an active role in His mission. He's just waiting for us to respond.

Growing up in the church, I somehow missed that message. I focused on the fact that Jesus loves me so much that He died for my sins. But I neglected to take a deeper look at the very reason He did it. Yes, it's because He loves me. But it's also because He has a goal to achieve, and I'm a part of His workforce. You are too.

We all are.

That means the real question is not *if* or *when* we'll be called to serve; it's *how* we will serve Him—*now*.

To be a part of sharing His incredible love with those who haven't experienced it, we have the opportunity to use our unique, God-given skills, talents, resources, and gifts. We are equipped to tackle heart-wrenching issues like poverty and injustice by making choices about how we will use the abilities, finances, and time He's blessed us with. We can use these things for Him, or for ourselves. I've personally made the latter choice plenty of times, but I continue to work on it. Luckily, each day offers a fresh start to wake up and decide who I'm going to work for.

If you'd like ideas, tools, or suggestions for next steps as you journey toward a life that embraces your role in God's family, visit thefamilybusinessparable.com.

Acknowledgments

This book would not have happened without the help of many amazing people. First, thanks to you, for reading and sharing this book as a part of your journey of service to God's work in the world.

Thanks to Dave and Dita for ideas, words, and laughter. You're great friends, and you made this entire process an incredible experience.

Thanks to Linda, Jeff, Doug, and the Tyndale team for support and excitement, and to Kristin for the intro!

Thanks to Tom, Lorna, Dimas, Corky, Candace, Chris, Lindsey, John, Rogeria, Amber, Lucas, and Sarah for early reading and feedback along the way.

For organizing my life and guarding my time, a big thank you to Karina. Thanks also to Andrew, Ewout, John, Wim, Danielle, Janet, Daniela, Bryce, and so many others serving through OM, for countless conversations which fed this story—even if you didn't know it.

And most of all, to Belén, for being a living example of God's love for me.

ALL THE PROCEEDS FROM THIS BOOK GO TO:
Operation Mobilisation (OM.org) and
the **Mission Gap Project** (missiongap.org)
to inspire, equip, and connect Jesus followers
for God's work around the world.